S.A. POLITICS

UNSPUN

STEPHEN GROOTES

Published by Mercury
an imprint of Burnet Media

•

Burnet Media is the publisher of Mercury and Two Dogs books
PO Box 53557, Kenilworth, 7745
South Africa

info@burnetmedia.co.za
www.burnetmedia.co.za
Twitter: @TwoDogs_Mercury
Facebook: TwoDogsMercury

•

First published 2013
1 3 5 7 9 8 6 4 2

•

© Primedia Broadcasting 2013
www.702.co.za
www.capetalk.co.za
Stephen Grootes has asserted his right to be identified as the author of this work.

•

•

Distributed by Jacana Media www.jacana.co.za
Printed and bound by Creda Communications www.creda.co.za

•

ISBN 9780987043764

Burnet Media |

About the author

Stephen Grootes is the host of the Midday Report on Talk Radio 702 and 567 Cape Talk, and the senior political correspondent for Eyewitness News. He is also a senior contributor at the *Daily Maverick*. He lives in Johannesburg with his wife and children and hopes to one day be an unpublished science-fiction writer.

Acknowledgments

To those who've gone before me, Mandy Wiener for *Killing Kebble* and Alex Parker for *50 People Who Stuffed Up South Africa*, and Jenny Crwys-Williams for keeping up the pressure.

We all owe a great debt to the journalists who really get their hands dirty finding the facts and uncovering the scandals: Adriaan Basson, Sam Sole, Stefaans Brümmer, Nic Dawes, Mzilikazi wa Afrika, Stephan Hofstatter, Carien du Plessis, Barry Bateman, Alex Eliseev and the still dearly missed and supremely wonderful Mandy Roussouw. And to those who helped me directly on this book, Gaye Davis and Ranjeni Munusamy.

The person who really worked on this book is Tim Richman. A man who can edit entire manuscripts in one night, work magic with graphs and sidebars, and basically make a book happen out of nothing but words. Tim, my everlasting gratitude, thank you – and also to the team at Burnet Media, and those who assisted along the way, including Terry Crawford-Browne and Nick Muller.

To Redi Tlhabi, thanks for being such a good friend and for always supporting me. And Jonathan Shapiro, thank you for taking on those who you know will fight back.

To Branko Brkic, the man who started the *Daily Maverick*, the first person I wrote for, who was gracious enough to welcome me back, thank you for being the visionary you are.

Primedia has been an incredible employer for the last eleven years, giving me space to grow, resources to work with and incredible platforms. Thank you – and particularly to Katy Katopodis, who made me stick to political reporting when I tried to duck it. Katy, you were right.

Thank you also to Shaun Johnson and Sir Humphrey, for setting me on the road to political reporting.

I grew up with the slogan "life isn't fair" ringing in my ears, and in my case it's absolutely true. I have had the immense benefit of a wonderful family, with my parents Meiert and Marilyn and my brothers Pieter and Nick all keeping me on my toes and ensuring I had the confidence to stand my ground when necessary.

And, of course, to my wife Angela, and my two wonderful and mostly adorable children. For keeping me sane, laughing and busy.

To Angela, without whom life would be supremely dull.

CONTENTS

3

4

5

Introduction

South African politics is fluid. It moves quickly. So quickly that someone who appears to be in complete control can suddenly find himself recalled from the Presidency. It is also complex. So complex – with many different constituencies and organisations working in coalitions with each other, and then against each other – that the average voter out there would be forgiven for being confused by it, even intimidated by it, from time to time. Or even all the time.

We live in a country where many of the debates that should happen between different political parties out in the open are held within the closed-door processes of the ANC. As in politics anywhere, there are historical reasons for the strange ways in which our system works. Our recent history is more intense, more ridden with conflict and, quite frankly, worse than that of many other democracies. That means the debates we have now are more emotional, more difficult and carry more subtext than those in other places.

But there are also some certainties: the structures and processes that fit together and work in a certain way. This book is an attempt to try to explain the politics of South Africa and make it more accessible to the average voter out there by offering a broad overview of those structures and processes and how they work, and explaining who the important players within them are as we approach the 2014 national elections. Crucially, it also attempts to explain why those players behave in the way they do, and how the choices and decisions they make could affect us all in the future.

It is not, and cannot be, comprehensive. There are many people who play decisive roles in our democracy who are not in this book. Those who are featured are the people who dominate the South African political landscape towards the end of 2013, as campaigning for the 2014 elections begins. A year ago many of them would not have made the list. In a year's time there will be new people on it.

Politics, despite the best intentions of universities everywhere, is not a science; it is an art. It is the art of managing humans in the best possible way. History teaches us that due to the fact that politics is about humans managing humans, those humans tend to interpret the "best possible way" as the "best possible way to benefit ourselves". That is unlikely to change. Ever. And it means there are very few unassailable facts in politics. Facts are themselves political, and sometimes open to question. They're certainly open to interpretation. Jacob Zuma can at the same time be a liberation hero, the saviour of the ANC, the expression of the people… and a womaniser, someone apparently corrupted, someone who can't be trusted.

To quote Gwede Mantashe, it depends on where you sit.

Which means that this book is, by and large, a work of analysis. Someone else with the same set of facts could write a very different book. Zuma definitely would.

It also means that the predictions made in this book, and particularly those to do with elections, are in no way grounded in certainty or permanence. If the book were published a few months earlier or later there could well be significant changes. Similarly, the POWER: MORAL ratios that you will find throughout are not written in stone, and they will naturally ebb and flow over time; just ask the man referenced in the first sentence here, Thabo Mbeki. Or Zwelinzima Vavi, whose ratio has swung dramatically during 2013 (making his entry particularly tricky to write!).

Predicting elections without comprehensive polling data – which both the ANC and the DA have, but keep close to their chests – and estimating an individual politician's power is not a game in which you will bet your house. But it is important to try to give justifiable assessments that might shed light on our political landscape. They are also an attempt to start a conversation about who is more powerful than whom – which can be continued, especially on Twitter: @StephenGrootes.

All in all, politics is about humans. Which is what this book is about.

A note on power and moral authority

The Grootes Power Rating ratios that you will find in this book are an attempt to measure a politician's real power against the moral authority he wields in society. In the first instance, the emphasis is on actual power to influence the course of South African politics. In the second, it is on moral authority as perceived by the public, rather than morality, which is a very different thing.

GROOTES POWER RATING ™

In South Africa, as in most places, the two can be quite different and can change over time, often dramatically. In British politics, for example, Tony Blair was once all powerful and had a high moral authority. After the 2003 Iraq War, he remained powerful but the moral authority had disappeared. Then, later still, so did the power.

Estimates of power and moral authority are, of course, subjective. The ones in this book were compiled in September 2013.

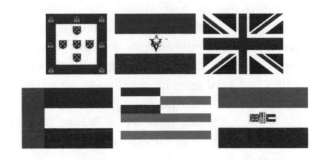

A brief history of SA politics pre-1990

Or: Why the ANC keeps blaming it all on colonialism/apartheid

Politics is about power. And those who have power write the history to control the past. In our case, that's truer than in most other places. Which is why for so long South Africans were taught that history started in 1488 when someone from Europe rounded the Cape and left behind a nice stone cross. But the actual first historical fact we have about our neck of the woods (after the fossil record, that is) is that our original farmers – or land-owners, if you like – came from East Africa around 280–550 AD. Point being you need to know a little something about South Africa's historical past to understand its current political present. And the first thing to know is that there are... multiple viewpoints.

So here's a thoroughly objective history of South Africa in a thousand words or less.

By 1075 the Kingdom of Mapungubwe was "the first class-based social system in southern Africa". A century later, Great Zimbabwe was the most powerful city-state in the area, making Cape Town's later claims to being "the mother city" infuriatingly Eurocentric.

It's probably fitting that the first white leader in South Africa was a corrupt official. Jan van Riebeeck had been bust trading for himself somewhere out east and, as punishment, was sent to set up a supply point at the Cape by the VOC, the world's first multinational corporation (so you know they had good intentions). Almost immediately, it seems, there was conflict with the local Khoi population; Van Riebeeck and his successors did not attempt to win them over with love. Before long there was a racial hierarchy going on in the colony and prisoners were being banished to Robben Island…

In 1688 the first French Huguenots arrived, ensuring that Springbok rugby teams would forever include names like Le Roux and Du Plessis, and by 1779 conflict between white settlers and Xhosa farmers became almost routine, leading to our very own Hundred Years War.

But the white groups kept fighting amongst themselves over who would run the place, with the Dutch and the English tribes not really agreeing on anything. Around the turn of the 18th century the English tribe won that particular war (and now we all speak English, innit?). Not long after, Shaka was king of the Zulus, which, depending on your point of view, led to some fighting and genocide or a complex migration of people through the interior of the country. End result: the Matabele moved to Zimbabwe and the Boer republics were set up in the Transvaal and Orange Free State.

WAR / CULTURAL DISAGREEMENTS

17TH CENTURY
Dutch v Khoi

18TH CENTURY
Dutch v Xhosa
Dutch v British

By this stage, parts of the country already had a "hut-tax" in force, which compelled black people to work for white people. And already we had the start of what could be seen as apartheid in everything but name: separate living areas, different laws for different races, and general tyranny.

Nevertheless, it was the white-on-white violence that continued, seeing its climax in the Boer War, in which Britain tried to subjugate the Boer republics. If you were black, of course, your subjugation was pretty much guaranteed (unless you were part of King Moshoeshoe's Basotho in current Lesotho). Eighty thousand or so died during the war, but the books of the time didn't record the twenty-something thousand black deaths. The whites finally agreed to stop fighting in 1902, and created the Union of South Africa in 1910 – which they probably could've done without all the fighting in the first place, in which case maybe Dutchmen wouldn't call English folk *rooineks* to this day. (But then again maybe they would.)

In 1912 the South African National Native Congress was formed, in one of the first attempts to unite black people against white rule. Bad timing: a year later, the Natives Land Act was signed and, in the words of Sol Plaatje, every black person woke up the next day "not actually a slave, but a pariah in the land of his birth".

Worse was to follow. In 1948 the National Party came to power, with the idea of implementing a novel social-engineering plan they marketed as "good neighbourliness". Also known as apartheid. The Race Registration Act formalised racial categories, pencil tests were introduced, forced removals began, pass laws were instituted, families were separated, jailed, torn asunder…

WAR / CULTURAL DISAGREEMENTS
19TH CENTURY
Dutch v British
British v Xhosa
Xhosas v Zulus
Zulus v everyone
Zulus v Boers
Boers v British

The ANC started its Defiance Campaign, and grew in strength and numbers. In 1960 there was international condemnation of the Sharpeville Massacre. By 1964, Nelson Mandela and others had been sentenced to life imprisonment, and other leaders had fled the country. Terror and darkness stalked much of the land; for most people there was no freedom – of movement, of assembly, of speech. Just owning a picture of Mandela was a crime. The armed struggle started, sanctions were imposed, the townships erupted, PW Botha put in place a state of emergency...

By now the United Democratic Front was gaining momentum inside the country while the ANC's international anti-apartheid campaign

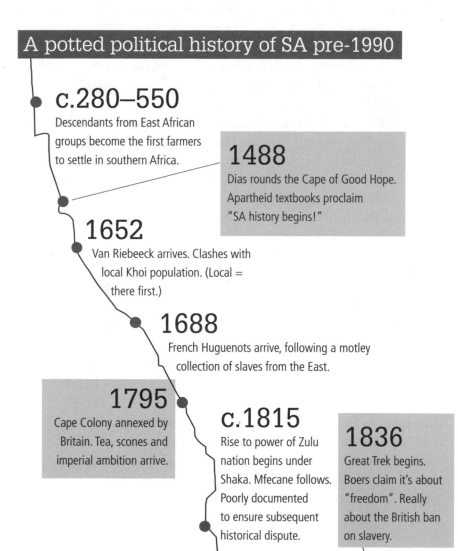

A potted political history of SA pre-1990

c.280–550
Descendants from East African groups become the first farmers to settle in southern Africa.

1488
Dias rounds the Cape of Good Hope. Apartheid textbooks proclaim "SA history begins!"

1652
Van Riebeeck arrives. Clashes with local Khoi population. (Local = there first.)

1688
French Huguenots arrive, following a motley collection of slaves from the East.

1795
Cape Colony annexed by Britain. Tea, scones and imperial ambition arrive.

c.1815
Rise to power of Zulu nation begins under Shaka. Mfecane follows. Poorly documented to ensure subsequent historical dispute.

1836
Great Trek begins. Boers claim it's about "freedom". Really about the British ban on slavery.

was beginning to bite on the global stage. The pressure was growing, and no-one really knew what would happen. Civil war, maybe? Imminent destruction?

Then, in 1990, FW de Klerk opened the prison gates, Mandela walked free, the ANC was unbanned. And there was political freedom.

POWER PERIODS

1488–1652 Portuguese (and European) explorations
1652–c.1800 Dutch colonial rule
c.1800–1910 British colonial rule
1910–1948 post-Union period
1948–1994 Afrikaner nationalists

1990
Liberation movements unbanned. Mandela's long walk to freedom ends (physically if not politically).

1986
Campaigns start to make the townships "ungovernable". State of emergency declared.

1976
Soweto Uprising begins, followed in 1977 by the murder of Biko in detention.

1948
Malan's Nats take power, offering a heady blend of racial "apartness" and police-state efficiency as a vision of the future. The apartheid apparatus kicks into gear over the next decade.

1960
69 people gunned down by police at Sharpeville, followed soon after by ANC ban.

1899
Boer (South African) War begins. Cue scorched earth, concentration camps and 80,000 dead.

1910
Union of South Africa comes into being. Smuts (prematurely) celebrates racial reconciliation – between Brit and Boer.

1852
South African Republic, a.k.a. Transvaal Republic, an independent Boer country, is established. Orange Free State follows in 1854.

A brief history of SA politics post-1990
Or: Why the DA keeps blaming it all on the ANC

Before Nelson Mandela walked out of jail in 1990, not many South Africans knew what he looked like. What they did know was the world around them was changing. Uncertainty reigned.

ANC exiles flew back into the country; Oliver Tambo, for decades gone from the land of his birth, arrived and then died a few months later; the ANC held its first conference at home since the 1960s, and voted Mandela leader. First talks about talks began, then more talks, then the Pretoria Minute, then the end of the armed struggle, then finally proper talks... And the temperature rose and rose.

KwaZulu-Natal plunged into ANC v IFP violence, and it emerged that the white government was giving the IFP weapons. Suddenly place names became synonymous with massacres: Boipatong, St James, Heidelberg. Then the assassination of Chris Hani, leader of the SACP. Two white right-wingers were arrested, and it seemed the end really was nigh. But Mandela went on TV (before De Klerk), gathered the nation in his arms and kept things together. No violence, he pleaded. We're nearly there.

Talks began again, and suddenly an election date was announced.

On 27 April 1994 we had a new flag, a new hope and freedom.

Then came the transition. Madiba wore the green and gold, FW left the Government of National Unity, GEAR economics started. Life changed.

By the beginning of the Mbeki presidency in 1999, it was time for transformation proper to begin. And that required very real changes to the country's power structure: affirmative action came into force and government policy started to change radically. Meanwhile, in Gauteng especially, violent crime moved from the townships and into the suburbs.

A second scourge, Aids, also took a terrible toll on the country. But Mbeki presumed to know better than medical science, and hundreds of thousands died unnecessarily (while Minister of Health Manto Tshabalala-Msimang received a liver transplant).

The Arms Deal was formally accepted by Parliament, and money started to make its filthy way into our politics in a big way. But the economy boomed and investment flowed in – partly because of demand for our gold, coal and platinum. From 2004 until 2009, house prices rose dramatically.

Inside the ANC, rebellion against Mbeki was stirring. When Jacob Zuma's financial advisor, Schabir Shaik, was convicted of paying him a bribe, Mbeki "relieved him of his duties". But ANC members refused to let Zuma resign as party deputy president, a sign of his strength and Mbeki's weakness. Then Zuma was charged with, and eventually cleared of, rape.

These tensions dominated our politics and the 2007 Polokwane conference saw its climax. Mbeki was out, Zuma in. Days later, Zuma was charged with corruption, but Mbeki had been compromised. The Nicholson

CRITICISM OF ANC'S POST-DEMOCRATIC GOVERNMENT

R30 billion+

"Irregular, fruitless and wasteful expenditure" by government departments during 2012, according to the Auditor-General.

R385 billion

Estimated total "stolen from poor people due to corruption" to mid-2013, as quoted by Mamphela Ramphele.

330,000+

Unnecessary or premature deaths due to the Mbeki-era HIV/Aids policy, as per a 2008 Harvard study.

50 Murders per day, a widely reported statistic in the mid-2000s.

judgment (later overturned) found that he may have interfered with the prosecution of Zuma. He was recalled, Kgalema Motlanthe put in charge for a while, and Cope was formed as a direct result.

In 2009 Zuma finally made it all the way to Number One, and Mbeki went to the Sudan. Zuma consolidated his power and the scandals rained

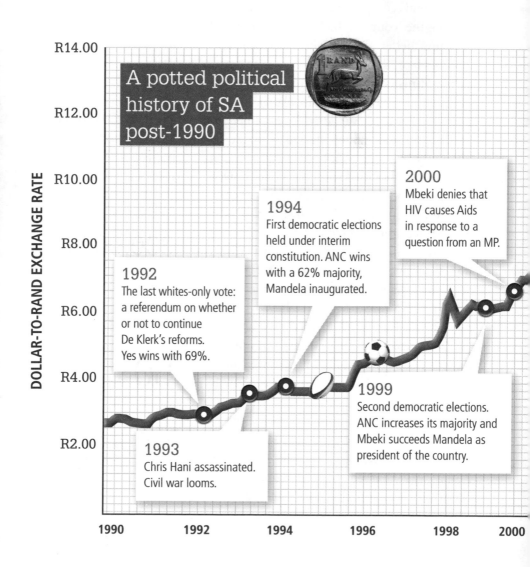

A potted political history of SA post-1990

1992
The last whites-only vote: a referendum on whether or not to continue De Klerk's reforms. Yes wins with 69%.

1993
Chris Hani assassinated. Civil war looms.

1994
First democratic elections held under interim constitution. ANC wins with a 62% majority, Mandela inaugurated.

2000
Mbeki denies that HIV causes Aids in response to a question from an MP.

1999
Second democratic elections. ANC increases its majority and Mbeki succeeds Mandela as president of the country.

DOLLAR-TO-RAND EXCHANGE RATE

R14.00
R12.00
R10.00
R8.00
R6.00
R4.00
R2.00

1990   1992   1994   1996   1998   2000

down. Bheki Cele, the Secrecy Bill, Richard Mdluli, the NPA, Nkandla... Julius Malema came and went. Tensions in the mining sector led to Marikana. But Zuma's power in the ANC was entrenched at the 2012 Mangaung conference, where he trounced Motlanthe.

And so we started to prepare for the 2014 elections, and beyond...

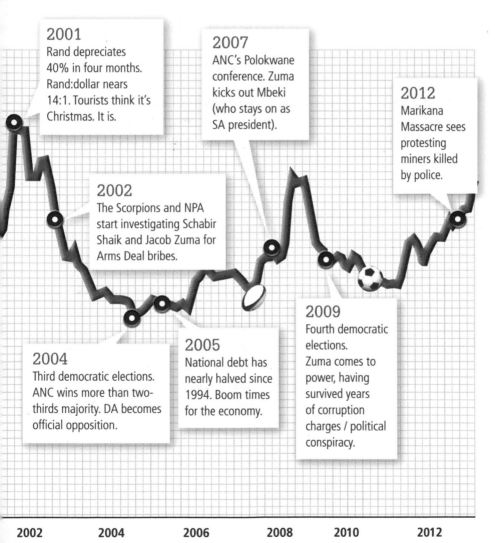

2001
Rand depreciates 40% in four months. Rand:dollar nears 14:1. Tourists think it's Christmas. It is.

2007
ANC's Polokwane conference. Zuma kicks out Mbeki (who stays on as SA president).

2012
Marikana Massacre sees protesting miners killed by police.

2002
The Scorpions and NPA start investigating Schabir Shaik and Jacob Zuma for Arms Deal bribes.

2009
Fourth democratic elections. Zuma comes to power, having survived years of corruption charges / political conspiracy.

2004
Third democratic elections. ANC wins more than two-thirds majority. DA becomes official opposition.

2005
National debt has nearly halved since 1994. Boom times for the economy.

2002   2004   2006   2008   2010   2012

The Constitution

Proclaimed: 1996

The supreme law of the land; our cherished guiding document and common ground; protection from the "tyranny of the majority"; a (historic) compromise and the basis of many of our fights – claimed by everyone (even though hardly anyone's read the thing)

Our Constitution hangs over us in so many ways it can be difficult to get a grasp on the thing. So allow me a personal anecdote.

On 10 December 1996 a friend and I drove to Sharpeville to watch then President Nelson Mandela sign the Constitution. It was one of the historic moments of our time, and we were in a minority; not many people at the Sharpeville stadium looked like us. As we made our way to the back to find seats, an organiser pounced on us, asking very politely if we'd like to sit on the field up front where we would have a better view. Immediately understanding that this was so we'd be caught in all our minority glory by international television cameras, my friend objected. Being less worthy than her, I insisted, and thus we got to sit in pride of place watching Madiba signing the most important document ever to receive a president's signature (at least in my mind).

The point to this is that the Constitution, quite deliberately, looks after minorities. It was the result of a compromise, negotiated when a white minority had control over the military and the economy.

A key aspect of this is Section 25, the Property Clause, which protects private property. It was a clause that would ensure that (most) white people got to keep their homes and swimming pools after 1994, while (most) black people would take generations to be able to afford those properties. Not exactly fair if you hadn't been allowed to vote before 1994. The other way of looking at it, though, is that the ANC realised that this element could not be negotiated away. No-one in power is going to just give away their property. Either the ANC compromised on this or the National Party would simply refuse to allow negotiations to continue, and would extend its apartheid governance for as long as its security and military forces could bear it.

Though its creation was never easy and could hardly please everyone, the Constitution is an amazing and wonderful document. It sets out how our country works. Critically, in the context of the modern political landscape, it explains that we, because of the compromises that had to be taken into account, have certain provisions that can only be changed if two-thirds of Parliament want to change them. This means that, for example, the Property Clause cannot be changed simply by one party alone – unless it wins more than 66.7 percent in a national election.

Rights

The most important aspect of the Constitution is that it grants every person in South Africa certain rights. You're born with these rights and they cannot be taken away from you for any reason. It's the Constitution that stands between humans being treated as humans – that is, humanely and properly – and, as the Constitutional Court likes to say, "the tyranny of the majority". For example, if right-handed people one day demanded that all left-handed people be culled (for whatever sensible-sounding or totally bigoted reasoning whatsoever), the Constitution would prevent this from happening. The lefties are safe. And for lefties, read any minority: whites, Zulus, Xhosas, Pedis, coloureds, Indians, gays, atheists, Jews, old people, the homeless, the disabled, the unemployed, prisoners, BEE executives, home owners, cyclists, Bovril-lovers, people who talk on their cellphones at the movies, whatever.

One of the Constitution's first declarations is that "everyone is equal before the law" (Section 9). In other words, you and I have the same rights as the president. It also points out that we are citizens, not subjects.

Everyone has the right to life. This is why we don't have capital

---

PREAMBLE TO THE CONSTITUTION
We, the people of South Africa,
Recognise the injustices of our past;
Honour those who suffered for justice and freedom in our land;
Respect those who have worked to build
and develop our country; and
Believe that South Africa belongs to all who live in it,
united in our diversity.
We therefore, through our freely elected representatives, adopt
this Constitution as the supreme law of the Republic so as to
Heal the divisions of the past and establish a society based on
democratic values, social justice and fundamental human rights;
Lay the foundations for a democratic and open society in which
government is based on the will of the people and every citizen
is equally protected by law;
Improve the quality of life of all citizens and free
the potential of each person; and
Build a united and democratic South Africa able to take its
rightful place as a sovereign state in the family of nations.
May God protect our people.
Nkosi Sikelel' iAfrika. Morena boloka setjhaba sa heso.
God seën Suid-Afrika. God bless South Africa.
Mudzimu fhatutshedza Afurika. Hosi katekisa Afrika.

---

punishment as a country – because the Constitution says we cannot.

Everyone has the right to dignity. So you can't, say, force a prisoner to live naked. But because of the limitation and balancing of rights, a prisoner can, with due cause, be strip searched. This constitutional point can also mean that, for example, the cartoonist Zapiro may not draw pictures of Zuma with a shower-head, unless he has a good reason to, because Zuma has the right to dignity. This balancing aspect is crucial to the way the entire system works, as not all rights are compatible with each other. In such a case – freedom of speech versus personal dignity – a decision eventually has to be made that effectively chooses between the two.

The Constitution sets out how our country and our politics work. It is the Constitution that says we are a proportional representation system of government – again, a compromise, to make sure minority voices are represented in Parliament. It is the Constitution that says we have nine provinces, and what their borders are. It's the Constitution that explains how our courts work in relation to our executive (government), and how Parliament works.

It is also the Constitution that places limits on power. So while it gives the president certain powers – for example, to appoint cabinet ministers – it also says he is not a de facto dictator. His choices and actions have to be "rational" and must comply with the

Concourt Case Landmark, 2000: Irene Grootboom

Informal settlement dweller Irene Grootboom went to court arguing that, under the Constitution, she had a right to housing, and that government must provide her with it. In 2000 the Constitutional Court eventually ruled in her favour, a case described by Judge Richard Goldstone as "the first building block in creating a jurisprudence of socio-economic rights". Essentially this means that government must house people if they can't do so themselves. Of course, this doesn't happen. Grootboom died in 2008, still without her house.

Concourt Case Landmark, 2002: Nevirapine

At the height of Thabo Mbeki's Aids lunacy, his government refused to provide the drug Nevirapine in state hospitals. It had been conclusively shown to stop women passing on HIV to their unborn children; they could even breastfeed with the drug. In 2002 the Treatment Action Campaign went to court to legally compel government to provide the drug, and were successful, resulting in the rare instance of a government being forced into an action. It was one of Mbeki's lowest moments but, to his credit, he did comply with the court order.

Constitution. You cannot appoint the worst person for a job when there are neutral criteria to judge who is the best. It is this part of the Constitution that allows organisations such as the DA to challenge, in court, some of what President Jacob Zuma does.

Why the Constitution is great

When the South African Constitution was signed into being in 1996 it was hailed around the world as a brilliant document, possibly the most progressive constitution in the world. And in a country that seems to be involved in a constant argument with itself, the Constitution is the one thing everyone seems to think is a good thing. It is the common ground. Generally speaking, this is because of the rights that it confers on people. Everyone likes having rights, and those rights are given to them by the Constitution; QED, the Constitution is good. In short, everyone knows that they can speak their mind in public because of the Constitution, and that it is this piece of paper that protects them when they get caught by the Metro cops after a long night's libation.

People who oppose the government, and particularly the ANC, like the Constitution because it gives them certain weapons and avenues for attacking or countering the ruling party. They also like the fact that it places limitations on Zuma's power.

The ANC and Zuma like the Constitution

because it gives them certain rights and powers, but also because it embodies so much of what the ANC fought for. It is, in large part, descended from the Freedom Charter of 1955, which is essentially the ANC's bible.

Why the Constitution is *not* great

Any system of government, or Constitution, is only as good as the people who work in that system. You can have a wonderfully democratic police service on paper, but if you appoint a drug dealer as its national commissioner, it's unlikely to be democratic in practice. So the Constitution can't protect you from the appointment of weak people to key positions. What it can do, though, is ensure those people are "fit and proper", which allows citizens of the country to legally challenge these appointments.

A major criticism of our system of government, and thus the Constitution, is that, due to our proportional representation system, party bosses get to select who becomes a member of parliament. Thus the only way to ensure that someone you don't like is not an MP is to not vote for that person's party. That may sound simple enough for some people, but for others, who perhaps have a certain history with a party, it can be very difficult. If our MPs represented certain geographic constituencies, goes the argument against proportional representation, then MPs would have to be accountable to those people rather than their party, and people with a proven record of corruption would be less likely to be elected to Parliament. But it's not that straightforward. In countries with constituency representation, such as Britain, many constituencies vote for a party more because of who leads it rather than who would represent that constituency.

Another criticism of the Constitution, which has emerged in the last few years, is that it gives people "too many rights and not enough responsibilities". This is an argument that's particularly pertinent to labour management; for example, when an employer wants to take action against an employee, it is partly because of the Constitution that it takes so long to get anything done. This is why someone like Jackie Selebi can be given a suspended leave of absence on full pay, leaving the country without a national police commissioner for a year and half; or why you can catch your store clerk with his hands in the till and, if you don't jump through exactly the right hoops in exactly the right order, you can't fire him.

Some of this criticism is valid, in that it makes it very difficult for anyone to manage an organisation (let alone government) if it's impossible to dismiss workers who aren't performing. In a historical sense, this over-protection is a natural reaction to the abuses of the apartheid era, when workers had very few rights, and hopefully it is temporary. In time, slow changes to the laws, and to the Constitution itself, should see some of these rights weakening slightly, allowing improved governance and business management.

Lost in interpretation

The Constitution is considered the root of all our other laws; any new law must stem from its principles and thus be compatible with it. Parliament cannot, for example, pass a law making it illegal to insult the president, because that would be incompatible with the constitutional right to freedom of speech.

But grey areas start emerging when you consider all the old laws that were passed long before the Constitution came into force. They, too, must be compatible. Common criminal laws – you can't murder, you can't steal, that kind of thing – are an obvious example of much older laws that are not constitutionally problematic. But what about the National Key Points Act, which has been on the books since 1980? Suddenly things are not so clear-cut, as debates arising from the Nkandla scandal illustrate.

Even though it may in theory be unconstitutional, an old law can still be enforced until someone goes to court – a High Court or above – and convinces a judge, or judges, that that's the case. That's why from time to time you hear debate about whether a law is actually legal or not.

While a lower court can determine if an action or a law is unconstitutional, the Constitutional Court is the final arbiter of all things constitutional. The buck (law) stops there, which is why this court is so important and revered.

Crucially, when passing judgment on what is or isn't constitutional, the Constitutional Court performs a balancing act. Rights granted to us as South Africans are important, but limited. Every right is balanced against every other right. Getting back to the Zapiro example, if you draw a cartoon of someone, your right to freedom of expression can be limited (in part) by the right to dignity of that person.

The court must also balance need with means. While it has ruled that everyone has the right to housing, it would be impossible for government to give everyone a house by lunchtime tomorrow. So it balances that need – the right to housing – with government's ability to give effect to that right.

Changing the Constitution

Usually, two-thirds of Parliament have to agree before a change to the Constitution can be made. For this to happen, either one party must have a large majority, or it must convince other parties to vote along with it – something that has already happened since

Concourt Case Landmark, 2012: Menzi Simelane
In 2012 the DA challenged President Jacob Zuma's appointment of Menzi Simelane as national director of public prosecutions. Eventually the Constitutional Court ruled that the decision was "irrational" and that there was an "objective test" of whether someone was "fit and proper". It was a major setback for Zuma, as it proved the limits of his power and meant he could be effectively challenged when making appointments and exercising his legal powers without complying with the law. *(See p215.)*

Constitutional Changes

Of the 17 amendments to the Constitution since its introduction in 1996, many have been technical, often to do with name or provincial boundary changes. Some other changes include:

- extending the cut-off date for deeds covered by the TRC (1997)
- making provision for party floor-crossing at various levels (2002/3), later repealed (2009)
- renaming the Northern Province to Limpopo (2003)

1994. In fact, it's happened seventeen times. Given the level of cooperation required, none of these amendments has been considered overly controversial. The concern for minority parties is that, should the ANC win a two-thirds majority (again), it would no longer need to consult with any of them to enact more controversial changes.

There are, however, parts of the Constitution that are much harder to change. Should it become necessary, for some reason, to curtail freedom of movement (say, when it's been raining for 40 straight days and nights and Noah's hearing voices again) or freedom of expression (when Lesotho's army is literally outside the Union Buildings), then Parliament can vote to do that. But it needs an overwhelming majority; in some cases more than 75 percent of the national vote, in some cases 80 percent. For obvious reasons, it's made deliberately harder than usual for our basic freedoms to be taken from us, but because it's impossible to predict the future there has to be some provision to change things, just in case the aliens from *District 9* really do arrive over Joburg one day.

It's important also to remember that not everything is a "constitutional" matter. For example, the debate over the powers of school governing bodies to limit the number of children in a class is a constitutional issue on one level, as it goes to the powers of government and whether it has to provide everyone with the right to a quality education. But government could simply change the law in

Parliament if it wanted, as the law on this is not a constitutional clause; it's simply a law. As we've seen above, though, that law could then be tested against the Constitution.

The Constitution in our current politics

As the Constitution effectively lays out the playing field of our politics, it is common for political parties and other political actors to try to claim some kind of ownership of it. In its basest form – and there's nothing as base as a politician fighting over the rules of the game – it's easy to imagine a Helen Zille or a Gwede Mantashe shouting, "Na-na na-na na na, the teacher's gonna get you." In other words, if you can show that "the Constitution is on my side" you look more South African, more right, and generally better in the public sphere.

This is particularly useful for the DA, which has used the constitutional limits on government power, and particularly on the powers of President Jacob Zuma, to great affect. Whenever an argument ends up in court with the judges agreeing with the DA, it makes the ANC look bad and the DA look good. And the ANC – or government – is forced into a position where it has to back down to avoid being unconstitutional and looking like a bully.

In recent years we've started to see a counter argument to this approach, claiming that people who use the Constitution to limit the power of government do so against the express will of the majority of the country. The label they've given this accusation is a lovely bit of politico-speak: "anti-majoritarianism". Because the majority voted for the ANC and it is the ANC in government that is trying to do something, it is "anti-majoritarian" to try to stop the ANC from doing that.

Without too much of a stretch of the imagination, "anti-majoritarian" can then be seen as a political code word for "racist", in that the majority of the people are black and they voted for the ANC, thus to stop the ANC from doing something is racist. And once again the race card is at play in SA politics.

The real problem with this argument, however, is that it's little more than a veiled attempt to wiggle around a fundamental aspect of the Constitution. The whole point of the document in the first place is to ensure that no one party, particularly government, has too much power, and that the rights of everyone, not just the majority, are protected. (Not surprising, then, that the person who seems to use the phrase the most is Blade Nzimande!)

Rather than blaming the Constitution directly and looking like a bully, a better approach – in the sense that it, at least, isn't obviously unconstitutional – is for the ANC to blame the people who do the interpreting; in other words, the judges. This is why there is such a ruckus whenever new judges are appointed – because if you can control the interpretation of the Constitution, in a way, you control the Constitution itself.

Likely future

Whether ANC, DA or "other", all political parties try to claim that the Constitution is on their side, and they always will. The upshot of this is that, while the document itself is unlikely to change in any major way for the foreseeable future, the fight over what it means and how it should be interpreted is only going to grow more intense. As perceptions grow that the Judicial Service Commission is appointing weaker judges who have the final say in constitutional interpretation, this may well become one of the defining battlegrounds of our politics in the coming years.

Elections

The time when we get to decide who really rules us; the democratic process; your chance to have a say; your duty as a citizen

Elections are the one time when ordinary South Africans get to cast a ballot; when they vote for whomever they want to lead the country. Don't get too excited now. As in most other countries, you get to choose from a very limited sct of options, the result of our (inevitably flawed) electoral system and the dynamics of the country itself. Most importantly, though, you get to help arrange the playing field for the next five years, and determine how much power those in power will actually have. South African elections are both a logistical triumph and the epitome of democracy in action.

How elections work: getting started

National elections are called by the sitting president. As per the stipulations of the Constitution, he has to call them within five years of the previous national elections, unless there is a state of emergency in place (and even then there is a limit on how long they can be delayed). The president thus already has some influence over proceedings; by determining the date, he can pick a time that best suits his party. In our context, 27 April – Freedom Day – is always a likely contender because it commemorates the ANC's finest hour. That said, there has to also be sufficient notice; a president can't just announce an election for tomorrow.

At the moment, South Africa has its national and provincial elections on the same date. There has been discussion within the ANC to change this, by including local government elections too. There are strong arguments each way. On the one hand, it would be cheaper and easier to have one election. On the other, people tend to vote in exactly the same way in both the national and provincial elections; if local government polls were held at the same time it's likely this trend would apply there as well, and thus local issues might not receive the attention they deserve. (If the ANC tries to go the three-in-one route, they will need to pass it through Parliament with a two-thirds majority, after which it will need at least five years to align the electoral cycles.)

Once the election is called, things in the land… change. First, everyone goes slightly mad. Then every single issue there is, from your views on inflation targeting to the quality of your poo-throwing, becomes election fodder. As campaigning starts, rules kick in for broadcast media, which ensure that there is equitable coverage of the various parties; they are not based on an equal formula, but rather on the results from the last election, so smaller parties don't get the same amount of coverage as the ANC or the DA, but they do get some. Just before voting actually starts, broadcast media are no longer allowed to actually cover reports of campaigning. This is why it appears as if the nation enters a twilight zone the evening before an election; everything stops, and there's a blessed silence after the cacophony of months of election campaigning.

How elections work: into the action

All elections are formally controlled by the Independent Electoral Commission, the members of which are appointed a bit like judges: parties get to nominate candidates, there are public hearings, and so on.

The IEC itself is a marvel. The only organisation that comes close to it in South Africa in terms of efficiency and getting the job done is the South African Revenue Service. If you think about what the IEC has to do, it's not a job for the faint-hearted. You have to arrange for every

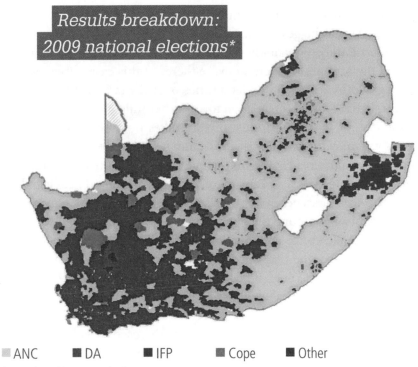

**Results breakdown:
2009 national elections***

■ ANC   ■ DA   ■ IFP   ■ Cope   ■ Other

*Map adapted from www.elections.org.za

single South African adult who wants to vote to be able to cast a ballot in exactly the same way, all over the country, on the same day. Fairly straightforward in Sandown and Constantia, but pretty tricky in the rural Eastern Cape or KZN.

To do this, the IEC goes to communities, finds people who are considered trustworthy by those communities, and appoints them as electoral officers. They are trained and paid, and given the power to run the voting booths themselves. In doing so, they make decisions on the ground, hold media interviews and basically run the show. It's completely different to the usual political arena, where ordinary party members are told to shut up and the flow of information is tightly controlled.

South Africa's biggest polling station, by number of people served, is at Joubert Park in Johannesburg. More than 5,000 people living in the flats in the area are registered to vote there. In this case, three separate polling booths are set up, under a series of IEC gazebos. The man who runs it, Patrick Phosa (no relation to any other influential Phosa), works at the City of Johannesburg usually but takes time off to work for the IEC. By 5am on the morning of an election he'll already be there, making sure everything's ready. The first queue normally forms an hour later, and when voting starts, at 7am, there are several hundred people in line. There are similar scenes in informal settlements around Gauteng, and in all the rural areas around the province.

Voting is allowed to continue until around 7pm, when the counting starts. Even then, the IEC will try to ensure that people already in the queue are allowed to vote. If necessary, the police, or even soldiers, will surround the queue to allow those in it to vote, while stopping anyone else from joining that queue.

Votes are counted at the polling stations themselves. Political parties are allowed to have representatives there to ensure that everything is kosher, and they get to watch the counting. By this stage everyone's been awake for over 24 hours and they can get a little nuts. It's common to see representatives from the DA and the ANC, who've been slagging each other off for months, sharing chairs and phone chargers and generally becoming friends. For just a few short hours.

The nerve centre of this counting operation is the IEC headquarters, normally at the Pretoria Showgrounds (now the Tshwane Events Centre), where every single political leader worth his or her salt goes to watch the massive scoreboard in the front of a cavernous hall. TV and radio stations usually fight for the best space, but the brilliantly organised IEC manages to keep most people happy. They also employ magical IEC fairies who provide three meals a day – and one in the middle of the night! – for everyone working there, most of them getting by on no sleep whatsoever.

With every national political leader there, it's also a chance to mend a few fences after the mud (and poo) throwing of the last few months.

The nerve centre is there to collate all the results as they come in. Using the IEC's computer system – which is made available on the web at www.elections.org.za – you can see not just the national and provincial results, but how people voted in individual polling stations. If you drill down through the data far enough, you actually get a scan of the document signed by the electoral officer for that station. This means that you can extrapolate not just how a party did across the country or even in regions, but how it did in very specific areas. This is how it was possible to work out that the ANC almost lost the vote in Port Elizabeth during the 2009 national elections, which meant the party knew it had to campaign very hard there in the 2011 local government polls.

As the counting continues, it usually becomes pretty obvious by the afternoon after the elections what the final outcome is going to be, and how much the ANC has won by. While the numbers on the scoreboard swing back and forth for a while, it should be clear within 24 hours what the majority will be and how much the playing field has changed.

At some point the IEC stops the scoreboard and then starts to prepare for its final announcement. There is some careful choreography here. The chair of the IEC makes the final announcement and then hands over the results of the election to the president of the country. This all takes place at one podium. The president goes through the ritual of thanking the IEC, appearing all very presidential in the process. Then the entire show shifts to another stage, where the president, now wearing his ANC leader hat, gives a completely different speech. It's one of those moments when protocol is very important. The president has to represent the country at one moment, the winning party at another.

When the counting is finally over, it's time to work out how it all translates into seats in the National Assembly and the National Council of Provinces. This is done according to a mathematical formula that sees around 20 million votes cut down to 400 seats in the National Assembly.

It can boil down to quite minute percentages at times, but the formula is supposed to favour the smaller parties ever so slightly to give them a better chance at representation and thus increase diversity.

To contest an election, each party has to provide the IEC with a list of 400 names of people who would represent it in Parliament should it (hypothetically...) win every vote in the country. Within the bigger parties it's hugely important for ambitious politicians to get on that list, and there are some rather vicious fights within the ANC and the DA over how the process works. If you're not high enough you won't become an MP, and then you can't become a minister either. Once the seats are allocated to the lucky 400, the country's new MPs then go through to Parliament where they will represent their parties in the votes that follow.

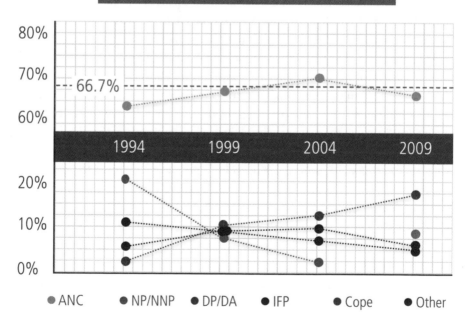

National election results since 1994

ANC   NP/NNP   DP/DA   IFP   Cope   Other

Parliament and beyond

The first time the new MPs meet in the National Assembly they hold a vote for the role of president. As our politics currently stands, this is a formality; everyone knows that the face next to "ANC" on the voting ballot is certain to be the country's next president. Still, candidates are nominated and a contest is held, with MPs voting loyally according to the party line. So if the ANC wants Jacob Zuma to be president, Jacob Zuma becomes president. Only when the winning party receives less than 50 percent of the national vote – perhaps when Jesus comes again – will this parliamentary vote hold any actual drama.

This is the real end point of the general election process. Once a person is elected president by Parliament, he forms a Cabinet and everything moves on from there.

Bring on 2014

As a general rule across Africa, the longer the fight for independence and freedom, the more people vote in elections. In South Africa we saw nearly 20 million people, almost every eligible person, voting in 1994; the numbers came down substantially after that, to less than 15 million in 2004, but rose again to 17 million in 2009. The current trends are seeing more and more black voters not bothering to go to the polls, while more and more minority voters are taking the trouble to vote (mostly for the DA). On one level this looks like simple dissatisfaction with the ANC, but it's more complicated than that and also has to do with a perception that the ANC is going to win anyway.

Predicting elections is asking for trouble. But give us a moment, and we'll get there. First, here are the trends that matter.

The 2014 national elections will have a lower turnout than those before. If you live in a rural area, you will probably vote for the ANC, and Jacob Zuma. If you live in an urban area, it's more complex; you may vote for the ANC or you may not. It seems hard to believe that support for the ANC in general, and Zuma in particular, has grown in urban areas in the last five years. That could well lead to a decrease in votes for the party. The other massive variable comes in the form of the one million people who voted for Cope in 2009: will they vote for them again, or for Agang, or possibly the DA?

Now, let's take the plunge:

The Stephen Grootes 2014 National Election Predictions*

	2009 result	2014 prediction	
ANC	65.9%	61%	▼
DA	16.7%	24%	▲
Agang	n/a	3%	▲
Cope	7.6%	3%	▼
IFP	4.5%	3%	▼
NFP	n/a	2%	▲
ACDP	0.8%	< 1%	■
EFF	n/a	< 1%	▲
FF+	0.8%	< 1%	■
UDM	0.8%	< 1%	■

*See individual party entries for explanations.

This prediction comes with a health warning. This is not a science. And when you get it wrong, as one almost inevitably does, the result is less than artistic.

Bear in mind that elections are that time when the differing focuses of various parties comes into play. The ANC talks up its history, its great leaders of the past, the fact it liberated the country, etc etc. The DA tries to claim it's the party of the future, that its service delivery record is better, its T-shirt's sexier, and so on.

It's an election. Don't believe everything they say.

Parliament

Motto: We, The People

South Africa's legislative body; the place of the people; where the power of the ANC finds full expression; where stuff is supposed to get done; a comfortable sleeping place

How it's supposed to work

You vote. It's counted. Based on the number of people who vote for a party, that party gets a certain number of members of parliament (out of a total of 400). They vote for and against certain laws that are proposed by the parties. Thus, the power flows from the people to the MPs who have been elected, who then create (and sometimes repeal) laws on behalf of the people. A beautiful, simple process.

As logic dictates, the party with the most votes has the most power. If it gets more than two-thirds of the votes, it then has even more power because it can now change parts of the Constitution – hence the focus during vote counting on whether the ANC will hit the magic 66.7 percent.

MPs are also supposed to ensure that ministers are called before them, in portfolio committees, to explain what their departments are doing. Thus Parliament is supposed to be a "check" on the "executive" (which is a legal way of saying the president and ministries, or the people who actually are supposed to act and govern).

All very straightforward, in theory; modern democracy in action.

What really happens

The ANC has by far the most players in the scrum that is Parliament. As a result, power actually flows from the people of South Africa to Luthuli House, where the ANC bigwigs either – depending on your viewpoint – try to change the country for the betterment of its people, or try to look out for the interests of the ANC alone and good governance be damned.

It works like this. A minister has certain problems in her ministry. Say, Basic Education Minister Angie Motshekga is battling with getting textbooks to schools in Limpopo. MPs are supposed to call her in and give her a real grilling to force her to explain what has gone wrong. There's that democracy in action again, right?

Ah, no. What you have, actually, is an ANC minister being called before a committee of MPs, the majority of whom happen to be from her party. With all the will in the world, it's hard to ask them to really take her apart on the hugely complex task of moving books from one place to another.

But it depends on who's involved. From time to time, you'll get an MP – who has his own agenda, usually involving his own personal advancement – who simply is the *moer* in with a particular minister.

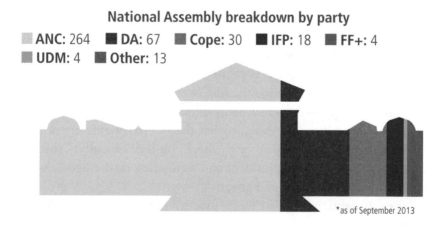

National Assembly breakdown by party

ANC: 264   DA: 67   Cope: 30   IFP: 18   FF+: 4
UDM: 4   Other: 13

*as of September 2013

In which case he will completely lose it and inform said minister in suitably parliamentary language where exactly to get off. One-time Communications Minister Dina Pule found this out the hard way, being repeatedly told to go away, sort her stuff out, then come back and try again. When she was fired in July 2013, it came – corruption allegations notwithstanding – as no great surprise to observers of Parliament.

Sometimes it's the opposition MPs who lead the charge; sometimes it's ANC MPs who get annoyed with their own ministers. Which is proof that pitting people's egos against each other really works in the long run.

The National Assembly

The workhorse of Parliament; where things really happen

There are two houses of Parliament. The National Assembly is the one on TV where you see MPs either shouting or sleeping, and it deals with national laws, involving things like the Police and Justice. This is where our laws are really debated and usually introduced for the first time. That's why you may have heard of it as the place where all the controversy about the Protection of State Information Bill began.

 AWOL MPs

An often-asked question about Parliament is, Where are all the MPs? The benches sure look empty much of the time… Due to the ANC's dominance, not all of its MPs need to be present; if a vote were held, it would still win. But the DA has managed to delay legislation on occasion by removing its MPs to ensure there's no quorum, so a vote can't be held. The person with the real headache is the ANC chief whip, who often has a lower party ranking than the people he's trying to discipline. You try telling Winnie Madikizela-Mandela what to do… Absenteeism has become so problematic that plans have been mooted to track MPs with electronic "cattle tags".

Party discipline

In 2011 two ANC MPs, Ben Turok and Gloria Borman, objected to the passing of the Protection of State Information Bill and, in a rare display of parliamentary dissent, abstained from voting on what Turok later termed an "obnoxious Bill". (He claimed he absolutely had to go to the loo at that very moment.) The ANC quickly declared that their behaviour "smacks of ill-discipline". But they were never publicly disciplined, mainly because no-one has the guts to take on Turok when he's right. It's a rare example of MPs not complying with their party's rules in the National Assembly.

The National Council of Provinces / NCOP

Fierce guardian of provincial interests; place of slumber and contentment

The National Council of Provinces is, as the name suggests, responsible for the provinces; it's where provincial interests in the national political sphere are considered. Major changes can technically be made to proposed laws when they arrive at the NCOP for further debate, which makes it really rather important, in theory. But in reality, because of the way the ANC is able to control MPs, the system has become one of... no-one really doing anything. So the NCOP hardly ever makes any meaningful changes to Bills, and tends to wallow about as a fat burden on taxpayers. (The contentious Info Bill was an exception – there big changes did happen – as was the Traditional Courts Bill, which some provinces strongly disagreed with.)

The real reason for this is that, due to the workings of our electoral system, you end up with exactly the same proportion of ANC / DA /other party MPs in the NCOP as in the National Assembly, and so any argument would mirror what's already happened in the National Assembly. The political parties themselves realise that it's far more worthwhile putting their better people in the National Assembly, with the result that their second-raters end up in the NCOP – which is even further motivation to steer clear of Bill changes here. To prove this point, the speaker in the National Assembly is ANC royalty Max Sisulu and the leader of the opposition is the DA's rising star Lindiwe Mazibuko. Name their equivalents in the NCOP if you can...

Could it change?
Absolutely. The MPs in the NCOP are ambitious, too, and it's not beyond them to decide, one day, that they actually want to assert themselves. (To a degree, this is what happened with the Protection of State Information Bill.) But any real change will be up to the initiative of the MPs themselves; to do this, they need to get out there, harness more media attention and catch the eyes of their bosses as much as they can.

The law-making process
Before a law becomes a law, it has to be proposed. This is usually done by the department itself. So its officials, led by the cabinet minister in charge, identify the need to change the law, to make said department run better and provide the country's people with a safer / better / more legally protected quality of living, or because the ANC has recently held a lekgotla at which it was agreed that a new law is required to achieve its latest policy ambitions. Once the Bill is passed by Parliament, it still has to go to the president to be signed into a law. But there are several hoops to jump through before that point.

First, the department produces the draft policy, also known as a Green Paper, and holds consultations on it with affected parties. This results in a fresh draft, known as a White Paper, which then goes to either the National Assembly or the NCOP, depending on whether it affects provincial powers or not. It's at this point that the relevant parliamentary committee will take over and discuss it. Usually, public hearings are being held by this point as well. Once the committee is happy – that is, it holds a vote to decide that the Bill is ready to move on (obviously with more representatives on the committee from the ANC than from

Why Cape Town, man?

There is no earthly reason why Parliament is still in Cape Town, and it is an unnecessary burden on the tax payer. The original decision was taken in the interests of "racial conciliation", back when only the Afrikaans and English races mattered. After the Boer War, a bone was thrown to each of the former players. Thus the Transvaal Republic got Pretoria as the administrative capital (and the Union Buildings); the Orange Free State got the Supreme Court of Appeal in Bloemfontein, and the Cape Colony got Parliament in Cape Town… And the Natal Colony got what many thought it deserved. Nothing (effectively).

other parties) – it goes to the main house, where a debate is held. Once passed, it must go to the other house to be voted on there. And then it goes back to the original house to check the changes. Changes can be introduced at all points during this process – which can drive everyone concerned to tears, to the point that they sometimes just tear the whole blasted thing up and start all over again.

Usually, MPs have to vote the way their parties dictate. But under certain circumstances, they will be allowed a "free vote" to vote according to their conscience. So those who are particularly opposed to abortion, for instance, might not be forced to vote in favour of it. At other times, parties impose a "three-line whip", which means that they absolutely must be there – no sickies, no loo breaks – and they must vote in the right way.

What happens next?

Once a Bill is passed through the two houses of Parliament, it then goes to the president, who has a constitutional duty to sign it into law. Generally, this happens quite quickly, but every now and then there can be delays. He can, as Jacob Zuma did with the Protection of State Information Bill, object to parts of it and send it back to Parliament. He can also send it to the Constitutional Court for it to be checked. And just to add to the delays, the Bill has to be translated from English into one of the other official languages. But the English text is usually the text that is considered final.

Once a Bill has been signed, it then gets published in the *Government Gazette*, along with the official date it comes into effect. And then it's the law. And don't you dare break it. Or forget your e-tag.

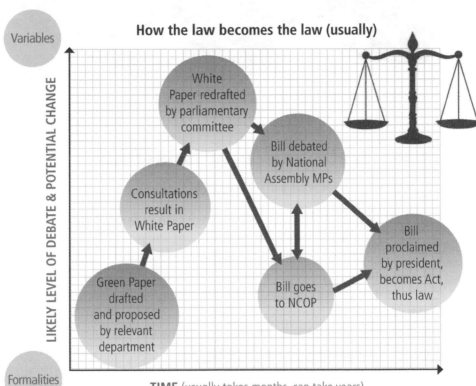

How the law becomes the law (usually)

Variables

LIKELY LEVEL OF DEBATE & POTENTIAL CHANGE

White Paper redrafted by parliamentary committee

Consultations result in White Paper

Bill debated by National Assembly MPs

Green Paper drafted and proposed by relevant department

Bill goes to NCOP

Bill proclaimed by president, becomes Act, thus law

Formalities

TIME (usually takes months, can take years)

National government   Provincial government   Local government

South Africa

Northern Cape

Upington

National, provincial and local government

The various hierarchies of power; why we care about some MECs and not others; who really has the power

The distribution of power at national, provincial and local levels goes to the heart of our constitutional and governing system. As part of the Codesa compromise, some powers under the Constitution are reserved for national government, some for the provinces and some for local councils. This means that in some areas the buck really does stop with the national minister, in others with a provincial MEC (basically a provincial minister), and in others with your local mayor. It doesn't always seem to make sense. But then compromises often don't.

National government powers

Being the MacDaddy of our system, the national government has the ability to create the country's broad policies and make laws. Crucially, it also gets to tax. As it controls the tax-raising functions, it means it has the most money, and the capability of getting more money when it needs it. This means it has the most power. And with power comes control over the parts of government that really matter. Particularly to government.

National government has a lot of theoretical power, as well as firepower power – which is to say it runs the army and police. Our safety and protection, both as individuals and as a country, is in its hands.

Departments like Police, Justice, Defence and Home Affairs sit with national government. These ministries have huge power, and are able to make the decisions that really matter. In summary, you might say that national government handles the "daddy issues".

Provincial government powers

Provincial governments don't have many revenue-raising powers. They are able to levy taxes on things like car licences (which is possibly the only reason you have to pay for a licence disc every year) and casinos, but they are pretty much dependent on national government for most of their money, which is paid based on a complex formula. This financial hold over the provinces allows national government to get hard and heavy, should it need to, to ensure that provinces toe the line.

Provinces are left with powers over what you could call the "mommy issues". The main departments they control are Health and Education, and this is why you will often see these particular MECs in the media so much; they are the people who run departments that actually matter.

Even then, they can't get too carried away. They are supposed to follow national guidelines and policies, which means they can't just run off and do their own thing in a way that is completely different to other parts of the country. Beyond that, in practical terms their powers are limited by the fact that the majority of provincial budgets go to schools and hospitals, both of which need large numbers of workers; so around 80 percent of their budget is destined for staff costs. Ultimately, even an important MEC's role can be disappointing and frustrating; it may look like you have some power, but you have limited room to manoeuvre.

Provinces do have some limited law-making power. For example, Gauteng has decided that bottle stores can be open on a Sunday; the Western Cape has decided they can't. They can also set certain regulations – different to laws – and thus certain issues can be interpreted differently from province to province. Children in South Africa usually go to schools based on geographical zoning, for instance, but KwaZulu-Natal has experimented with a first-come, first-served system.

Local government powers

Local government means your local council, the people you pay your lights and water bills to. Technically they get their money both from national and provincial government, and then also from your rates and levies. In other words, they receive money for the services they (are supposed to) provide.

They also have the power to set by-laws. So they can decide at what time on a Saturday night you really *really* have to turn off your Eminem.

How they relate to each other

There is a dedicated ministry, the Department of Cooperative Governance and Traditional Affairs – previously the Department of Provincial and Local Government – to oversee the relationships between national, provincial and local governments. It is, of course, run from national government, so the hierarchy of power is quickly apparent.

The minister in question has certain powers relating to appointments and the behaviour of provinces and councils, so if a province is not performing properly – for example, if school kids still don't have textbooks halfway through the year – he can legally intervene.

This can be hugely controversial. You can imagine, for example, the fun and games there would be should a national ANC minister try to intervene in a DA provincial department in the Western Cape. To add to the high jinks there are several different types of intervention on offer, ranging from a sort of "intervention lite", involving national officials being sent to assist a province, to the full-scale "intervention hard and heavy", in which national government actually assumes responsibility of an entire department. When this happens, as it did to five Limpopo departments in 2011 – where else? – the national minister actually becomes, legally speaking, the MEC for that department in that province, with all the relevant powers. But don't think it always works. National government has taken over the Department of Education in the Eastern Cape several times since 1994, and it's still the official definition of disaster.

Similarly, provinces have an MEC for Cooperative Government who has the power to intervene in local government if necessary. So if a council is taking money from people, but has cocked things up so much that there is raw sewage flowing from your taps, the province can decide to take over.

Despite the tangled and unsatisfactory situations that can arise from the interactions between the different levels of government, the final analysis is relatively straightforward: the councils are weak, provinces are a little bit stronger, and national government is the strongest.

Possible changes

As the rights of national government, provinces and local councils are set out in the Constitution, it seems unlikely they will change any time soon. While the DA would like the provinces to have more powers – because they run the Western Cape – the ANC would, unsurprisingly, prefer them not to. Should the ANC try to weaken the provinces and steer even more power towards national government, you can bet the DA will be in court faster than you can say "outrage".

The Judicial Service Commission

*The body that appoints our judges; the focal point of
our most pressing social debates; a shaper of our future;
South Africa's controversies personified*

The Judicial Service Commission is one of those organisations that seems to do nothing but create controversy. If it had a quiet uncontroversial meeting it would generate a headline as earth-shattering as WINNIE MADIKIZELA-MANDELA ARRIVES ON TIME. The JSC's main job – in effect, its only job – is to interview and recommend people to be appointed as judges by the president. It sounds simple. But then so does finding the Higgs boson.

Here's the thing: if you can appoint the judges who will hear all the controversial cases in the future then you can win all those cases. But, you ask, would politicians ever stoop that low? Surely not!

In a word, yes. Remember: he who controls the Constitutional Court, wins. It's that simple.

But those clever people who wrote the Constitution realised this. And so there were huge fights at Codesa as to how judges would be appointed. In the end a typical grand South African compromise emerged.

The old, white, generally male judges could stay. New judges would be appointed – but not by the Justice minister as had been the case in the past. The Nats knew they'd managed to jimmy that system, and they weren't about to let someone else do the same thing. So the JSC was proposed as a buffer of sorts. It has politicians on it, to ensure the elected voice of the people is represented, but also a nice mix of other people.

THE CONSTITUTION SPECIFIES THAT
THE JSC CONSISTS OF:

The chief justice
The head of the Supreme Court of Appeal
A provincial judge president selected by the other judges president
The Justice minister
Two advocates nominated from the advocates' profession
Two attorneys nominated from the attorneys' profession
One law academic
Six MPs from the National Assembly, of whom three must be from opposition parties
Four people from the National Council of Provinces
Four people appointed by the president

What this means is that the Constitution has intentionally created an inherent bias against the government, the idea being that the JSC cannot be dominated by the ruling party of the day. The ANC has, however, used its majority in the National Council of Provinces to ensure, over time, that all four of these representatives are its members – and they follow orders to the letter. (Legend has it that two of them have simply never spoken during JSC meetings!)

Then we have the representatives of the advocates and the attorneys – the former being general lawyers, the latter being specialist lawyers. These two groups have politics as spectacularly complicated as the inner workings of the Large Hadron Collider. As a result, each of these bodies ends up nominating one white member and one black member. Sad, isn't it?

And there's the man at the centre of it all, Chief Justice Mogoeng Mogoeng. His is the crucial role. As chairman, he gets to set agendas and, importantly, chair the interviews of judges. So, if he doesn't like one of his fellow commission members' questions, the candidate doesn't have to answer. And if he wants to give someone a grilling, he can go to town.

But the key figure in the current JSC has actually turned out to be Minister of Justice Jeff Radebe. You can tell immediately from what he has to say whether he likes someone or not. And you know that everyone will fall in behind him.

In 2009, just after Zuma had ascended to the Presidency, the JSC interviewed more than twenty candidates for four positions on the Constitutional Court. It was the last time ever that four posts would come up at the same time, a once-in-a-lifetime opportunity to change the balance of the court.

Appropriately, the interviews took three days.

And the JSC made up its mind in under three hours.

It is simply not possible to weigh up the merits of twenty candidates in three hours. This should have taken a week to decide. If anyone ever claims that the JSC is completely non-partisan and makes appointments based on merit alone, this is how you know it's not true.

Black and white decisions

The JSC has, time and time again, had to grapple with one major issue, a tension that is now out in the open.

In its simplest form, the argument is that most of the best lawyers available to become judges in South Africa are white men. But there are still way too many white men on the bench, so the JSC has a problem on its hands. The Constitution says that the judiciary must "broadly reflect" the racial and gender demographics of the country. This then must vie with the intention to also appoint the "best people for the job". In the media this argument gets boiled down to "merit" versus "transformation". Which is often bollocks, because you cannot say that Pius Langa or Dikgang Moseneke were not appointed on merit. They were simply the best brains in the country.

In practical terms, though, this is a tough balancing act, and it seems undeniable that the leading candidates are being passed over at a worrying rate. The perfect example of this is Jeremy Gauntlett, who is seen by many as the best advocate in the country (by miles). He has acted as a judge, and even as an Appeals Court judge in Lesotho and Swaziland, and is seen as superbly qualified. He's also damn funny when he's being interviewed. But the JSC has passed him over five times, dismissing his case with the explanation that he "lacks judicial temperament". What that means exactly hasn't been fully explained.

This issue is going to be tested by the courts themselves at some point. The JSC itself is subject to judicial review, and will eventually be taken to court by Freedom Under Law, an NGO itself headed by a former Constitutional Court judge, Johann Kriegler. Kriegler is the guy who oversaw the 1994 elections, so he has huge legitimacy. It will be an interesting case to follow.

Possible future

The JSC is going to come under increasing pressure, and the role of Mogoeng himself is likely to be hugely scrutinised – in the media and, ultimately, the courts. As the commission now stands, it's hard for a public observer not to believe that this is a group of people who are, in the main, operating as one voice rather than a collective of differing viewpoints – and thus the JSC is at good risk of losing legitimacy in the eyes of the public. Your average man in the street probably doesn't care about the race of the judge overseeing his trial; he just wants a fair hearing. But judges are simply too powerful to be left to their own devices by politicians, so don't think for a moment that the ANC is likely to give up any of its influence here.

Chief Justice Mogoeng Mogoeng

Born: 14 January 1961
Chief Justice of South Africa; God's choice to head our judiciary

Judge Mogoeng Mogoeng is the head of arguably the most powerful section of our government, the judiciary. He doesn't just head the Constitutional Court – where he has only one vote out of eleven, like the other judges – he also chairs the Judicial Service Commission, and thus plays a guiding role in appointing new judges. His decisions will have implications for years to come in our country. And yet, until his appointment to Constitution Hill, little was known about him.

Up until 2009 Mogoeng was simply judge president of the North West. He was one of just six judges in the province. It had only thirty advocates. By contrast, the South Gauteng High Court has thirty judges sitting at any one time. During Mogoeng's 2009 JSC hearing for the position of Constitutional Court judge, he complained he'd been "left in Mafikeng" for too long and wanted to leave. His whole interview was, in fact, considered a bit of a joke; it was short, and he preached like the minister he is. But, in yet more evidence that an ANC-aligned group controls the JSC, he was appointed. Two years later, Jacob Zuma suddenly decided Mogoeng should be chief justice. Cue the sort of outrage only Zuma can provoke.

With gay-rights activists to the left, supporters of Deputy Chief Justice Dikgang Moseneke to the right, and the usual anti-Zuma campaigners all about, Mogoeng was stuck in the middle of the biggest judicial ruckus in years. Part of the problem was that he had dissented in a case relating to images of homosexual sex and hadn't provided his legal reasons for doing so (as he is compelled to by law). He had also dissented in a defamation case involving that most controversial of policemen, Robert McBride, and written that "dignity" and "freedom of expression" carried equal weight. Which, as it so happens, they do not.

But the main claim against him, fairly or unfairly, was that he was a judicial lightweight, someone with very little experience who wasn't really up to the job, and he was being appointed by Zuma simply because he was the judge who had the most similar attitudes to Zuma. You know, towards gay people, women, on social issues generally and so on…

Then there's his religion. During his JSC interview for the post of chief justice, he was asked if God wanted him as chief justice. His answer, "I think so", probably sums up his sense of self-worth and his religious views quite neatly. And there's the problem. The Constitution doesn't mind judges being religious so long as their first duty is to the Constitution. But Mogoeng is a member of a holy fire-breathing brand of reborn religion that sometimes seems to suggest a duty to Christ overrides everything else.

Likely future

To date, Mogoeng has made no hugely contentious judgments as chief justice, and he has plenty of critics looking closely for them. But he is in this job until 2021, guaranteed. He literally has to die or go to jail to be replaced before then. The quiet won't last. At some point there will be a huge controversy involving him and possibly his beliefs.

The Presidency

*The office of the president; the apex of our governing system;
where Zuma goes to work; a place with good lawyers*

Despite the fact that it is in charge of the entire country, the Presidency is actually not that large a department. It is situated in the Union Buildings in Pretoria, which is where Jacob Zuma goes to work most mornings. When in Cape Town, he goes to Tuynhuys.

Technically, the Presidency includes four "political principals": the president, the deputy president (currently Kgalema Motlanthe; doesn't have much to do these days), the Planning minister (Trevor Manuel) and the Performance minister (Collins Chabane). While they don't all share an office, they probably do bump into each other at teatime.

There is of course administration that needs to be done, and inevitably lawyers and advisors ("the Legal and Executive Services unit") also need to be employed to make sure everything the president does is good and properly legal. The person who really seems to call the shots in Zuma's office is Lakela Kaunda, who's been one of his closest aides for many years.

The main jobs in this office include running Zuma's day-to-day affairs, communicating on his behalf *(see Mac Maharaj, p66)* and, with involvement from International Relations, sorting out protocol issues.

Jacob Zuma

Born: 12 April 1942

*President of South Africa; president of the ANC;
Commander-in-Chief; Number One; the man in charge; the
unstoppable tsunami; the come-back kid; the walking controversy*

No matter what you say about Jacob Zuma – and plenty of people have
plenty to say – everyone would at least agree that he is someone who
evokes strong emotions. You either love him or you hate him. There is very

Timeline

1959	1963	1973	1974
Joins ANC, ANCYL and SACTU.	Jailed for 10 years for political activity.	Released from Robben Island.	Establishes underground ANC structures in KZN.

POWER　MORAL

GROOTES POWER RATING ™

little middle ground. And the reason for this is that Zuma is the person who most polarises our nation, along various lines at various times.

Sometimes it's along political lines. "The ANC will rule until Jesus comes" is something that could have you ululating with joy or foaming at the mouth. His behaviour during *The Spear* saga, which involved the Lenin-esque image of him naked and a little more than tumescent, either made you glory in the celebration of the protection and reverence of your culture or had you weeping for your lost artistic rights.

Understanding JZ

The reason for this polarisation is simpler than it sometimes appears. Like all of us, Zuma is a product of his upbringing, and then his life experiences in the struggle. From rural KwaZulu-Natal, he was brought up single-handed by his domestic-worker mother. Both the Zulu language and Zulu culture run deep with him. Zulu speakers say his use of the language is like no other. And, like no other South African politician before him, he is able to get a crowd not just dancing and singing, not just emoting and thinking, but actually feeling as if they are with him on stage.

At the end of the Mangaung conference that saw him re-elected as ANC president in December 2012, he announced in his final address

1986	1987	1993	1997
Involved in Operation Vula in KZN.	Appointed head of ANC Intelligence.	Plays major role in ending KZN violence.	Elected ANC deputy president.

that Nelson Mandela was coming out of hospital, then he led the crowd in an old ANC song and, as the music climaxed, he stopped and said (what's been translated from Zulu as), "I don't know what it's like outside, but here in the ANC, it's good." The party faithful lapped it up.

To be a follower of Jacob Zuma is not just to adopt his views and attitudes, and to shake your head in sage agreement with his policy pronouncements; it's to *believe* in Jacob Zuma. He is the embodiment of something else, of a culture that has been trampled on, abused, kicked around for all too long. When he was jailed by the apartheid state he didn't bend on Robben Island; he came back for more, taking important roles within the ANC in exile and then running Operation Vula in KZN. If he'd been caught, it might have been tickets permanently.

When he was accused of rape and then corruption, people massed not just to protect him, but also to protect the most powerful symbol they had of themselves. They too had been abused by the legal system. Zuma's message was pitch-perfect: "If they can do this to me, then imagine what they can do to you." It is unbeatable politics in modern South Africa; there is no way to fight it, and that's why Zuma is so powerful now.

The bad, the good and his greatest skill

It is impossible to analyse Zuma unemotionally. A major part of his appeal is in fact his emotional pull, and most people who try to analyse him make the mistake of deconstructing his words in English. That's not

1999	2002	2005	2006
Becomes deputy president of South Africa.	Implicated in Arms Deal corruption, with Schabir Shaik.	Fired as deputy president of South Africa, but not ANC.	High-profile rape trial. Eventually acquitted of charges.

the point of Zuma. The point of the man is that he is able to understand how people feel. And then make them feel that much better because they are with him.

Of course, Zuma doesn't make everyone feel better. He makes certain parts of South Africa feel downright ill. These are the people who will never feel comfortable with him in charge, who think that emotion has no place in politics, that Zuma has repeatedly proved himself as simply bad and a liability for the country.

To find a middle ground is difficult.

The litany of complaints about Zuma is virtually endless. Schabir Shaik, his corruption trial, his rape trial, his wives, his affairs, the spy tapes, the judges, Nkandla, Waterkloof, the Guptas… Then there's the endless secrecy about everything and – what now seems to be absolutely true – that he will use our spies against us. These are very serious problems, all of which have in some way harmed our nation and our society. The damage Zuma has done to our criminal justice system alone might take generations to fix. How do you justify taking eight months to appoint a head of the National Prosecuting Authority? How can you remove the head of the Special Investigating Unit and not appoint a new one for eighteen months? And how, with tears in our eyes, can you spend more than R200 million rand of our money on Nkandla and then claim you knew nothing about it? *(See Controversies!, p201.)*

It's insulting.

2007	2009	2012	2013
Elected as ANC president at Polokwane.	Becomes president of South Africa.	Nkandla scandal.	Waterkloof scandal.

Then again, we must remember the country where we came from: Mbeki's South Africa, riven by the HIV/Aids scandal, an unacknowledged crime scourge and endless debates about race. These are now under control, barely talking points.

By simply appointing the best possible people in the health sector and allowing them to shift to a sane, scientific approach, our Aids epidemic has changed from being a tragic worldwide embarrassment to the example of global best practice. Almost everyone who needs them is getting life-saving antiretroviral drugs, and all indicators have improved enormously in just five years since Mbeki ruled. *(See p202.)*

Gone are the days of ANC ministers saying that if you don't like crime then leave the country. In its place we have a far more pragmatic attitude to crime, involving more police officers and what seems to be action. (Marred, of course, by a shoot-to-kill attitude and a brutality that is just mind-bending.)

And then there's race. It's hard now to imagine it, but there was a time when every rugby or cricket team announcement would lead to arguments about quotas, when every sports selection was a political story. Zuma has almost removed race from our national discussion. Not entirely of course – this is South Africa – but we remember our divisions less than we used to, because he doesn't feel the need to bring them up all the time. And in that alone he has done something very few other people would have been able to do.

Zuma is sometimes accused of not acting, of not being direct in his speech, of always skirting the issue and never actually answering the question. To a point that is correct; he is not someone who will give you a straight answer to a straight question. But we must not judge him against his political colleagues here; rather we must judge him against other heads of state, none of whom gives simple answers to simple questions. That's because when it comes to being president, it's complicated; you often need to be very careful when you speak. And if you're Zuma, a man who has a long history of being treated by our media in a certain way, then you *always* need to be careful. So when he gets asked how he decided who to appoint to the NPA, his answer will be, "I applied my mind". And when that's followed up with, "What do you mean by that?", his answer again will be, "I applied my mind." You won't get any more.

That said, when he feels the time is right, he can be very direct in his speech. Both Cope and Julius Malema have felt the anger of his tongue when it's aroused.

The polarising president

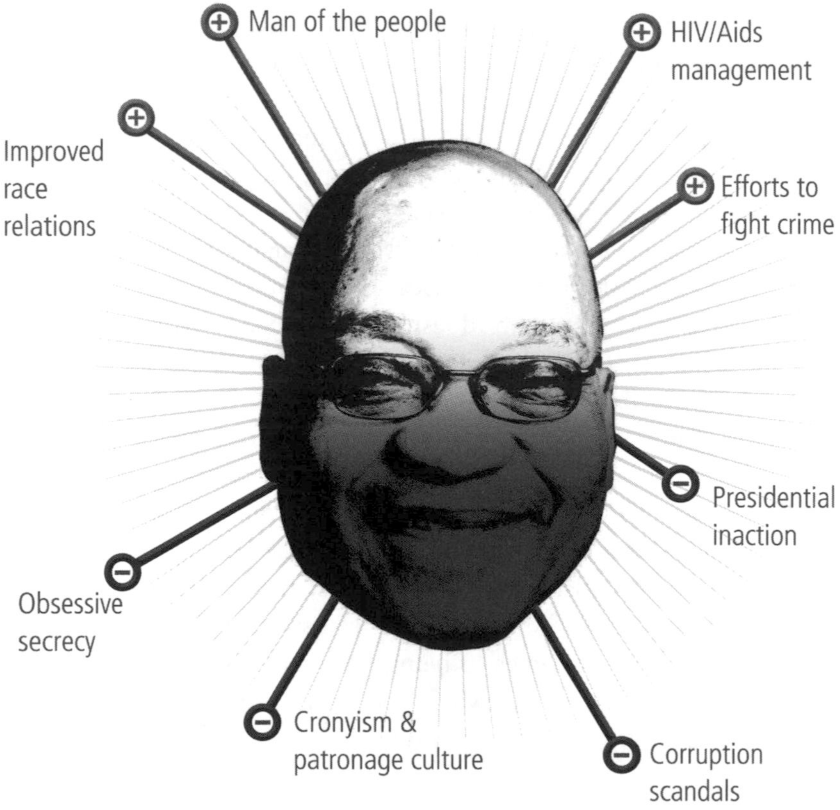

⊕ Man of the people

⊕ HIV/Aids management

⊕ Improved race relations

⊕ Efforts to fight crime

⊖ Presidential inaction

⊖ Obsessive secrecy

⊖ Cronyism & patronage culture

⊖ Corruption scandals

It's also a mistake to judge Zuma by Western media standards. He does not give a speech like Barack Obama because there is no political reason for him to do so. We are not a television democracy. It's understandable to get frustrated when listening to him trudging through his annual State of the Nation address every year – soaring oratory, it sure ain't – but making setpiece speeches (in English) is not a priority for Zuma. He didn't need to be good at them to get in to power, or to stay there.

Instead he needed to arrange the structures of the ANC in the way that best suited him. And in this he has succeeded better than anyone before him. This is partly because of a previous position he held: chief of ANC Intelligence. It's a job you don't get by being stupid or cowardly. Instead he went up against the best the National Party had to offer and, as history has shown, he ended up on the winning side. Two decades later he has the trust of, or dirt on, the people who count.

The man of mystery

Much has been written about Zuma and his personal life, but a large amount of it is difficult to substantiate or pin down. A memorable line in one of his biographies notes that he married Nkosazana Dlamini-Zuma "some time in the 1980s". A polygamist, Zuma has been married six times in total. One wife committed suicide, while Dlamini-Zuma divorced him in 1998. If you ask him how many children he has, you will not get an answer, but it's thought there are twenty or more young Zumas running around, not all produced from the sanctity of his marriages.

In person Zuma can be kind and thoughtful, and he's full of stories about the ANC. It is often in the past that he feels most comfortable, and he can hold forth for hours about how he and a group of youths were disciplined for planning violence in the streets of Durban, or about the time he and Thabo had to jump over the same fence to get out of Swaziland. (Yes, that's Thabo Mbeki; they used to be pals.)

As an ANC leader, Zuma is currently feted and praised wherever he goes by the black, green and gold faithful. But official ANC histories may

How to address him: "Mr President."

His answer to a tough question: A laugh.

Favourite gesture: Pushing his glasses back up on to his nose with his middle finger.

not remember him so kindly. Because many of the actions Zuma has taken to strengthen himself may well have weakened the party in the long run. Just his election and his decision to allow Mbeki to be recalled led to the split-off (and subsequent running joke) that is Cope. His re-election at Mangaung may well lead to the splitting of Cosatu and the eventual weakening of the ANC as well. His ejection of Julius Malema from the party has led to the formation of the Economic Freedom Fighters and his tolerance of corruption helped to create Agang.

It is not entirely fair to blame all of this on him. The country was changing and developing anyway, and Malema, for example, is the consummate loose cannon (if he is the consummate anything). Still, if you're the leader when you hit rough waters, you should at least give the appearance of trying to steady the ship.

Likely future

Having won re-election to the presidency of the ANC at Mangaung, Zuma seems certain to stay on as president of the country after the 2014 elections. But his power is likely to start ebbing halfway through his second term as attention moves to the race for his successor and what's likely to be another headline-grabbing ANC conference in 2017.

While power is one of Zuma's priorities, another may well be staying out of jail. After his financial advisor Schabir Shaik was convicted of paying him a bribe in 2005, Zuma was formally charged with corruption. Eventually those charges were withdrawn *(see p218)*, but the spectre of them still lingers. For Zuma to be properly free of them, he needs to control the National Prosecuting Authority in the short run *(see p215)*, and cut some kind of deal with his successor as president not to prosecute him in the long run. Like Vladimir Putin, Zuma runs the risk of becoming a hostage to power. If he leaves office, can he trust the person who comes after him not to reinstate those corruption charges? If he can't, well, then he's in a bit of a dilemma.

This feeds nicely into the question of who he would like to succeed him, and whether he will actually be able to influence that appointment anyway. He picked Cyril Ramaphosa to be his running mate for Mangaung, thus ensuring he became deputy president of the ANC. That immediately led to speculation the ANC might want to somehow manoeuvre Ramaphosa into the presidency in 2014, rather than Zuma. That seems hugely unlikely. Why would Zuma give up power? There would be nothing in it for him, even if his critics claimed it would boost the ANC at the polls.

Mode of address to female reporters: "My dear."

Favourite meal: Oxtail, then rooibos tea with honey (no alcohol).

Favourite song: Really, you don't know this one?

The most likely outcome is that Ramaphosa will be appointed deputy president of the country, which would be an indication that Zuma wants him to take over in 2019. If not, then the other likely contender is his ex-wife, Nkosazana Dlamini-Zuma.

Once Zuma does leave power, and supposing the corruption charges don't re-emerge, he will probably simply retire to Nkandla, and stay there. It's highly doubtful he would be seen as a moral paragon for people to aspire to, and he would be unlikely to seek to play any roles on a diplomatic level. Sadly, given that we're living them now, it's hard to imagine that most people will long for the days when Zuma was in charge.

Mac Maharaj

Born: 22 April 1935

Presidential spokesperson and spin-doctor-in-chief; Zuma's greatest defender; political force of nature; tainted liberation hero

For most people now, Sathyandranath Ragunanan "Mac" Maharaj is the man who simply defends President Jacob Zuma and does nothing else. He's the guy who somehow thinks it's okay for the Gupta family to use Waterkloof, or for Zuma to spend more than R200 million – *our* R200 million – at Nkandla. But scratch the surface and you will find a world-

Timeline

1964	1987	1994	2003
Arrested and sentenced to 12 years on Robben Island.	Part of Operation Vula.	Appointed Transport minister.	Discredited by Hefer Commission.

class political operative with a history that any liberation icon would envy. Famous among Robben Islanders for his ability to stand up to torture, this is the man who quite literally was in the cell next to Nelson Mandela. When he was finally released in 1976, he strolled out with a secret transcript of *A Long Walk To Freedom* on his person. That's right; without

GROOTES POWER RATING ™

Maharaj, there would be no award-winning movie now. And if he'd been caught, they would have sent him straight back.

Past

Maharaj was deployed to Zambia by the ANC, and won election onto its National Executive Committee in 1985. And then he went right back into South Africa, secretly, as part of Operation Vula. Unbelievably dangerous work, this was the bid to try to infiltrate some of the ANC's top leaders back into the country so they could mobilise more opposition to apartheid. Much of what you want to know about Maharaj's current position has to do with this one fact: he went underground, along with Mo and Yunus Shaik and Pravin Gordhan, and the person they all reported to was the head of ANC Intelligence, Jacob Zuma. Had they been caught they would have faced the worst kind of torture, and so they had to be hugely loyal to each other. It really explains the trust that Zuma has in Maharaj now.

After 1994, Maharaj went into Nelson Mandela's cabinet as Transport minister. At the time, transport wasn't necessarily the biggest issue, but some of the decisions he was involved with still have an impact on our society today. Under his watch, the legislation that makes it possible to operate an airline in South Africa only if you're a South African was pushed through, something that perhaps overly benefits SAA.

The damage to Maharaj's reputation as a proud struggle hero came, as it has with many, in the shape of Arms Deal allegations. Somewhere along

How to address him: "Hey, Mac." (Really.)

His answer to a tough question: "No, that's not the case. The president's lawyers are dealing with this…"

the line, people started believing, he'd taken money. There were then further allegations regarding tenders that arose during his time as Transport minister, with Schabir Shaik's name featuring prominently.

During the late 2000s it emerged that Maharaj had given evidence to the Scorpions, which seemed to implicate him in some form of bribery. His discussion with prosecutors is legally sealed and may not be published, but that didn't stop the *Mail & Guardian* from trying in 2011. When they did, he laid criminal charges against the newspaper and two senior journalists, and the story was pulled.

Maharaj has now got himself to the point where if you ask him outright, "Did you take money during the Arms Deal?", he won't give you a straight answer. And it really does seem that at one point Schabir Shaik put a rather substantial amount of money in Maharaj's bank account. Not in the Umlazi branch of Nedbank, but in Switzerland. Maharaj could argue that that was simply a gift, given the long-standing relationship he has with the Shaik family. But the allegations remain, and the *Mail & Guardian* was happy to publish details of numerous other suspicious payments.

It's a classic tragedy. A man who could quite realistically be called one of the superheroes of the struggle, brought low, we think, by the lure of filthy lucre.

In 2003 Maharaj was forced to testify at the Hefer Commission, which investigated allegations that then National Prosecuting Authority head Bulelani Ngcuka had been a spy for the apartheid government within the ANC. Ngcuka was the man driving the corruption investigation into Zuma, so it seems Maharaj had a political agenda here to protect his friend. By the time the commission finished, he'd been totally discredited in the public eye.

Present

In a move that was unexpected at the time – but makes complete sense, given a little thought – Zuma plucked Maharaj out of obscurity and made him his spokesperson in July 2011. It was a role that immediately thrust him back into the forefront of the media spotlight. Not a day goes by when you won't hear Maharaj in some way, shape or form.

As a communicator and a spin-doctor, he's absolutely world class. It's not easy to spin for Zuma, yet he does it well. He's one of the few people in the country who realises the value of the off-the-record chat, the background briefing that will inform a journalist's analysis and make sure that Zuma emerges looking as good as possible. He also realises there's nothing more a journalist hates than having to apologise in public; if a reporter has got something wrong, he explains the error off the record rather than demanding an apology. It's an approach that works, and is part of the reason so many journalists will give Maharaj credibility. Fact is, he's a professional. His phone is always on, he returns calls and he always knows exactly who he's talking to.

An added string to Maharaj's bow is that he's a real political player in his own right. He is still one of Zuma's point men on Zimbabwe, for example, and is the guy who literally takes a message from Zuma to Mugabe, and the response back to Zuma.

In person, and off the record, Maharaj is amiable, often brutally honest, and actually very funny. But, as you can imagine, he also has a temper and he's not afraid to use it.

Likely future

Even though Maharaj is now in his late 70s, there appears no sign yet that he's running out of steam. But it does seem that this job, as Zuma's spokesman, is likely to be his last. It's a pity. South Africa owes Maharaj a great debt. Certainly, he should be remembered more fondly than his current public profile suggests. He's been a great soldier for liberation and for freedom, and hugely loyal to his friend Jacob Zuma. Perhaps too loyal.

The Cabinet

Cabinet is to the country what executive management is to a corporation – but with one crucial difference. Whereas executives generally have some legal protection and can't be fired without due process, cabinet ministers can. The Cabinet is specifically exempt from labour law because the Constitution recognises it as a political entity. To be blunt, the Cabinet is really an extension of the president. He appoints cabinet ministers as he sees fit, and assigns their powers. They serve, quite literally, at his pleasure. Which might explain some of the stranger decisions we've seen ministers make; decisions that might endear a minister to his or her all-powerful boss. Otherwise, how to make sense of the reaction of the Public Works ministry to the Nkandla scandal, for instance? *(See p227.)*

Picking his Cabinet is one of the first major decisions of a president's term. There is, literally, a lot of politics involved, so it's not simply a case of best man for the job. For one, if you're the leader of a broad church like the ANC, with many factions, a complicated alliance and a recent history of strained national conferences, your own internal party dynamics are unavoidable. You have to both reward your supporters and keep your enemies sweet. This means people whom Jacob Zuma may not like that much have to get jobs. It also means that organisations like the SACP and Cosatu have to get a cut of the action. Thus, Ebrahim Patel represents the unions at Economic Development, while Rob Davies represents the SACP at Trade and Industry. Which is wonderful for party and alliance unity – but rubbish for economic policy (assuming you're wanting a coherent one that makes sense). It also means there is the temptation to expand the Cabinet, as Zuma has done. It makes life a little easier for the one in charge – but also means you have more ministers, more ministries and, inevitably, more BMWs being bought with public money.

Naturally, if you're president, placed there by the ruling party, you are unlikely to want to appoint ministers from other parties – unless there's a very good reason for it. Such as making yourself appear magnanimous and all-embracing. Which is how Pieter Mulder, the leader of the Freedom Front Plus came to be the current deputy minister of Agriculture. It's a neat trick – especially in this case, because Mulder gets to look after the farmers who make up a large portion of the FF+'s support base – but such appointments never end up in the really influential ministries.

Most cabinet ministers are members of parliament, but the president is allowed to pick two non-MPs. This is for special cases, when someone of real ability is needed. So FW de Klerk appointed Derek Keys, a financial expert but not a politician, as finance minister in the '90s. That tradition continues; current Minister of Finance Pravin Gordhan is also not an MP. But the Constitution does insist that the vast majority of ministers are democratically elected to Parliament. In other words, Cabinet has to represent, to an almost total extent, the will of the people.

Here follows a brief introduction to the various ministers in Jacob Zuma's Cabinet, as of September 2013. Four of the current government's major players feature first; the rest appear alphabetically by department. Of course some ministries are more important than others, and their budgets vary enormously. While often the budget determines importance, this is not always the case. The minister in charge of your spies (Siyabonga Cwele) can be more important than the minister in charge of your water supplies (Edna Molewa), even with a far smaller budget. See the following graph to get an idea.

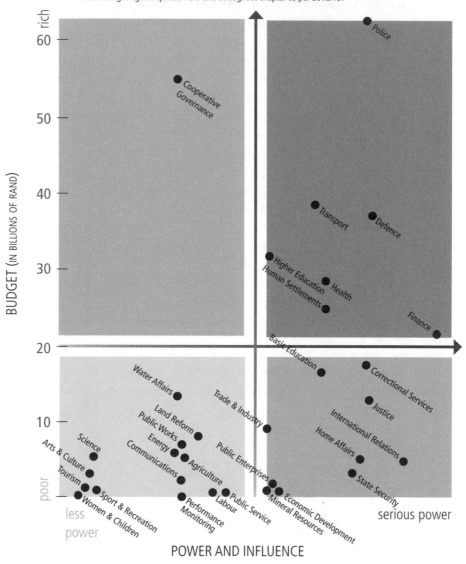

Cabinet departments: Power v Budget

Note: budget figures quoted here and throughout chapter as per 2012/13.

BUDGET (IN BILLIONS OF RAND)

rich

poor

Social Development (R112b)

Police

Cooperative Governance

Transport

Defence

Higher Education

Human Settlements

Health

Finance

Basic Education

Water Affairs

Correctional Services

Trade & Industry

Justice

Land Reform

Public Works

International Relations

Energy

Home Affairs

Science

Communications

Agriculture

Arts & Culture

Public Enterprises

Tourism

State Security

Sport & Recreation

Labour

Public Service

Economic Development

Women & Children

Performance Monitoring

Mineral Resources

less power

serious power

POWER AND INFLUENCE

Siyabonga Cwele
MINISTER OF STATE SECURITY

South Africa's spy master; champion of the
Secrecy Bill; remarkably unaware husband

Siyabonga Cwele is the man responsible for our spies. And, boy, does he have the wrong personal life for that. His ex-wife, Sheryl, is currently serving a jail sentence for drug trafficking, having groomed young women to smuggle cocaine. Her trial in the Pietermaritzburg High Court resulted in huge headlines, but silence from him. So we had a serving cabinet minister, in charge of people with access to fake passports, whose wife was selling drugs. Understandably, he claimed not to know anything about the whole fiasco, but that only led to claims that he's unfit for his job. Remember, he's in charge of knowing what people are up to…

Cwele, though, is very close to Zuma, and so seems safe. To be sure, he divorced Sheryl after the trial.

Formerly the chair of Parliament's Joint Standing Committee on Intelligence, Cwele's tenure as minister has been marked by the extended and hugely controversial battle over the Protection of State Information Bill. He is very much the man behind it, having driven it through Parliament, despite fierce countrywide opposition. In its original form, the Bill would have allowed anyone he designated to classify certain documents as secret, and if someone had published those documents they would face a 20-year jail sentence. So a man whose wife was running a drugs ring from his home wants the power to make government documents top secret… It's unclear how this would help fight corruption.

Though occupying one of the most important and powerful positions in Cabinet, Cwele clearly misjudged the public mood and was ultimately forced to make several concessions to the Bill. *(See p220.)*

(See p220.)

8 1
POWER MORAL
GROOTES POWER RATING ™

Likely future

The fact that Cwele is still in Cabinet has more to do with his relationship with the president than any competence for the job, so expect him to move on if and when Zuma does.

Pravin Gordhan
MINISTER OF FINANCE
The voice of prudence within government; the man who pays the bills
Department budget R21.6 billion

In charge of the most powerful department in Cabinet, Pravin Gordhan is a former SACP member, who was very active in KwaZulu-Natal. As mentioned earlier, he was involved in Operation Vula with Zuma and Mac Maharaj during the '80s, which gives him considerable pull in today's government. It's clear that he still has Zuma's ear, and that when he makes certain pronouncements he knows his political back is covered. The other reason for his political confidence is that it would be very difficult for Zuma to replace him. Gordhan has a credible voice on the international stage and inspires confidence in the global business community. If he were to leave the position it's entirely possible the rand would lose substantial value. In other words, he has assumed Trevor Manuel's title and reputation.

Gordhan became finance minister in 2009 after a highly successful stint running the South African Revenue Services. He brought the reputation he forged during that time into his new role, and so got off to a good start. Since then, it's been his job to try to rein in government spending, an unbelievably difficult job, in large part because of the political promises made by his boss. Over time, he has created a reputation for prudence. (Quite famously, he ordered relatively affordable Audi and Lexus sedans while his fellow ministers went to town buying million-rand Mercedes and BMW limos during the outcry over ministerial vehicle expenses in 2009.)

Without much political fallout, Gordhan has managed to take over some of the financial decisions of government departments, creating a unit within the Treasury that monitors spending and can act when it feels overspending is happening. This has increased both his responsibility and his power. The fact that he's been able to do it is proof of his ability to fight political battles and win them.

Gordhan is one of those people who never says what he doesn't mean, and knows the absolute power of words. So when he says something will happen, it's because he absolutely knows it will. If he doesn't know it will happen, he won't say it.

He's a man who doesn't suffer fools, and is quite happy to answer a controversial question with a heart-crushing quip of his own. Like finance ministers anywhere, he has to deal with smart-alec questions from people who know very little, and can get a bit frustrated with it all. It's understandable, both because of the responsibility he holds and because he is probably the cleverest person in government, with a phenomenal memory. He once answered a question on live radio with the suggestion, "Why don't we consult our Constitution? I happen to have a copy here with me" – before citing page and paragraph number and the relevant clause. He didn't have it with him; it was all from memory.

Gordhan is not a man you want to be arguing against. If you are in government and you want to achieve something, get him on your side first.

Likely future

Until Mangaung in 2012, Gordhan wasn't a member of the ANC's National Executive Committee, which is unusual for someone in such a prominent government position. He is also not a member of parliament, as one of the two cabinet ministers the Constitution allows

8 8
POWER MORAL
GROOTES POWER RATING ™

the president to simply appoint.

Gordhan's place at Finance under Zuma seems assured, if only because the president doesn't have anyone else he trusts who can do it. Should Gordhan leave office, he's likely to get a job on one of the world economic bodies, perhaps at the United Nations.

Aaron Motsoaledi
MINISTER OF HEALTH
Healer of our broken health system; fixer of our wrong Aids policies; the most accessible man in Cabinet

Department budget R27.6 billion

If someone had to ask who had done the most for the country while in Jacob Zuma's Cabinet, Aaron Motsoaledi would be the guy with the big silver trophy. Almost a political unknown before 2009, he has been the person who has worked exceptionally hard at, and been exceptionally honest about, what needs to be fixed in our country.

In some ways he had it slightly easier than other ministers. After the damage wrought during the Mbeki era, and the public animosity shown towards Manto Tshabalala-Msimang, anyone who came into office promising antiretroviral drugs for people with HIV was going to be popular. And the fact that his boss agreed with him made it all that much easier. Still, the numbers are impressive.

Nearly 12 million South Africans have been screened for HIV since 2009, to go with public tests for Zuma and most of his ministers. Most government hospitals have stocks of ARVs to give free to people who need them. As a result, the life expectancy of an average South African has risen to about 60, from the lows of the mid-50s only a few years ago. This is a hugely impressive feat. *(See p202.)*

All this, and the man himself is an exceptionally nice person. Just about every journalist in the country has Motsoaledi's cell number, he answers it, and almost always tries to do what he can to help. When people die in hospitals through negligence, he turns almost purple he gets so cross. He insists on investigations and fires the people responsible.

GROOTES POWER RATING ™

If he could be cloned, we would have nations around the world banging on our door for copies of him.

Motsoaledi also takes care to be apolitical, working hard to improve health services for everyone. But Health being Health, he can be controversial. He's insisted on investigations into private health care costs, is pushing for a ban on alcohol advertising and is the minister tasked with introducing the disputed National Health Insurance scheme.

Likely future

Motsoaledi's future seems assured. He's likely to stay in the Ministry of Health for some time to come, mainly because he's got such a big job to do and he does it so well. But plans to ban booze advertising or place health warnings on fast food are likely to keep him in the headlines.

Jeff Radebe
MINISTER OF JUSTICE AND CONSTITUTIONAL DEVELOPMENT
Cabinet veteran; key to the JSC; power player
Department budget R13.1 billion
Jeff Radebe is South Africa's only politician to serve in every Cabinet since originally being appointed by Nelson Mandela back in 1994. Considering all

the changes within the ANC during that time, that's quite a feat. (Trevor Manuel comes close, having been first appointed in 1996.) And right now he probably wields the most power he has ever had, considering the current situation in the justice system.

Radebe joined the ANC while studying in the late '70s, before leaving the country on ANC orders. Arrested in the mid-'80s and accused of terrorism offenses, he was represented by the late Pius Langa, who was practising as an advocate at the time. (Radebe had grown up with Langa's younger brother.) He spent several years on Robben Island, and was released after Mandela in 1990.

Radebe was put in charge of Public Works in South Africa's first democratic cabinet, before moving through the portfolios of Public Enterprises, Transport and finally Justice. While at Transport, Radebe was made acting Health minister while Manto Tshabalala-Msimang recovered from her liver transplant. It seems he played a major role in pushing Mbeki to allow hospitals to provide antiretroviral drugs, under a new Aids policy he pushed through while she was still recovering. Good work, then.

At Justice, however, Radebe has been at his most controversial. He has been the front man for decisions taken by Zuma that appear to only weaken the justice system. He advised Zuma to appoint Menzi Simelane as head of Public Prosecutions, in a decision that was then struck down by the Constitutional Court. He has also appeared to watch from the sidelines as the NPA failed again and again to get convictions in high-profile crimes,

GROOTES POWER RATING ™

as in the Andries Tatane case. Some of the convictions it gets are almost unbelievably lame; for example, in the J Arthur Brown prosecution. He has also been unable to explain why Zuma refused to appoint a head to the Special Investigating Unit for nearly two years. As a result, Radebe has become the symbol of all that is wrong with the justice system under Zuma.

Radebe is married to Bridgette Radebe, a mining entrepreneur and sister of one of our richest citizens, Patrice Motsepe.

Likely future

As long as Zuma is in power, Radebe will be safe, it seems. But the role he's played in using (or not using) the justice system to protect Zuma is likely to come back to haunt him when Zuma goes.

(See The JSC, p50, and The dysfunctional NPA, p215.)

MINISTER OF AGRICULTURE, FORESTRY AND FISHERIES
Tina Joemat-Pettersson
Department budget R5.8 billion

Joemat-Pettersson has found it difficult to stay out of the news, following a trip to Sweden in 2010 that possibly was or wasn't a holiday. Urgently called home by the president, she spent more than R150,000 on flights for herself, her kids and the au pair. The Public Protector has suggested, rather strongly, that she repay the money.

More pertinently, her department has been in trouble over its inability to properly survey the fish in our seas, which means that our fishing industry could lose the right to export to the European Union, one of its biggest markets. Within the ANC she has also had to contend with voices calling for urgent land redistribution. She appears to have tried to reassure farmers that they won't lose land that is producing food.

GROOTES POWER RATING ™

GROOTES POWER RATING ™

MINISTER OF ARTS AND CULTURE
Paul Mashatile

Department budget R2.7 billion

Mashatile is the leader of the ANC in Gauteng, one of the few provinces that voted against retaining Zuma at Mangaung. As such, he's one of Zuma's most powerful public enemies, someone Zuma would probably prefer to remove from office if he didn't fear the reaction from the province. Mashatile is hugely popular in Gauteng, having led the province for many years, but he has been passed over for the post of premier, which he's always craved. He is still angry about it.

At Arts and Culture – one of the less revered ministries, to put it kindly – Mashatile has done well to keep out of the disputes that can arise when our culture is discussed, and was one of the (few) sober ANC voices during *The Spear* controversy in 2012.

He has been accused of being a member of the "Alex Mafia", a group of ANC politicians from Alexandra. The claim, which has not been legally substantiated, is that this group benefits from tenders in the province.

MINISTER OF BASIC EDUCATION
Angie Motshekga

Department budget R16.3 billion

Motshekga is the minister South Africans love to hate at the moment. She's had to carry the can for the Limpopo textbooks disaster, which saw pupils there without books for the entire 2012 school year. This resulted in huge public outrage, with a multitude of calls for her head. Motshekga herself admitted that year that half a

GROOTES POWER RATING ™

million books ordered by her department had simply not been received, let alone distributed, while newspaper reports suggest that the "universal coverage" she had promised by 2014 just isn't going to happen. Then one of her officials signed a deal with the South African Democratic Teachers Union (SADTU) that saw teachers receiving increases she couldn't afford. Despite this, Motshekga appears to have Zuma's full support.

He is perhaps not entirely wrong about her, and she's received unexpected support from the likes of Helen Zille. With education a key priority for the ANC (and voters), Zuma believes she is the best person to make real change happen. That she is passionate about education is not in doubt, and she takes the time and the trouble to listen to people with other ideas, including those from independent/private schools. Equally doubtless is the extent of her problem. South Africa's education system is in dire straits, and was ranked 140th out of 144 countries in a World Economic Forum report in April 2013.

Motshekga comes from Gauteng, and was one of the first people in the province to campaign within the ANC for Zuma. No surprises, she's a close ally of his.

MINISTER OF COMMUNICATIONS
Yunus Carrim

Department budget R1.7 billion

Carrim was appointed to Cabinet in July 2013, taking over a department that has been helmed by a number of underperforming and/ or controversial ministers. Ever wondered why South Africa's internet speeds are more than three times slower than the global average? This is the department responsible, and Carrim's predecessor, Dina Pule, is currently

GROOTES POWER RATING ™

under investigation, having been fired by Zuma when boyfriend-related corruption and nepotism allegations emerged.

Carrim comes from the SACP, and has a reputation for hard work and wanting to get things done. He first hit the headlines when he headed the parliamentary committee that formally decided to abolish the Scorpions anti-corruption unit in 2009.

POWER MORAL
GROOTES POWER RATING ™

MINISTER OF COOPERATIVE GOVERNANCE AND TRADITIONAL AFFAIRS
Lechesa Tsenoli

Department budget R54.7 billion

Tsenoli was appointed in July 2013 to head the department responsible for managing the relationships between national, provincial and local governments. It may not be the most influential portfolio, but it sure comes with a massive budget – only Social Development and Police have more to spend – which largely goes as grants to municipalities around the country.

Tsenoli took over from the axed Richard Baloyi. Previously he had spent a long stint as deputy minister at Rural Development and Land Reform, where he had been a sober voice. Another SACP appointee, he came into front-line politics through the SA National Civics Organisation, and played a role in the youth politics of the 1980s.

MINISTER OF CORRECTIONAL SERVICES
S'bu Ndebele

Department budget R17.7 billion

Ndebele is the former premier of KwaZulu-Natal, where he had the distinction of being probably the only ANC member in that province

GROOTES POWER RATING ™

who backed Mbeki rather than Zuma at Polokwane. Despite this, Zuma offered him a Cabinet post in 2009. As punishment, it was the Transport portfolio, meaning Ndebele had public responsibility for road accidents. Zuma has continued the medicine by shifting him to Correctional Services; now he is responsible for prison escapes. Ndebele has kept relatively quiet in both departments, and is likely to try to stay below the political radar as much as possible for the time being.

MINISTER OF DEFENCE AND MILITARY VETERANS
Nosiviwe Mapisa-Nqakula
Department budget R37.5 billion

There was general surprise when Mapisa-Nqakula was given one of the country's key Cabinet positions – mainly because she did such a poor job at Home Affairs under Mbeki. She was also asleep at the wheel while leader of the ANC Women's League, not noticing that it was going to support Zuma in 2007, rather than her candidate, Mbeki.

Unfortunately, her reputation at Defence remains unchanged. One notable incident had her putting every military base in the country on alert simply because Julius Malema wanted to speak to soldiers at one of them. Her current strength appears to be that she follows Zuma's orders and does what he wants. But she is unlikely to advance any further in the ANC, or in government.

GROOTES POWER RATING ™

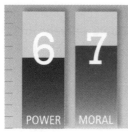

MINISTER OF ECONOMIC DEVELOPMENT
Ebrahim Patel

Department budget R700 million

Patel is a Leftie, with a capital L, and makes no bones about it. The former leader of the South African Clothing and Textile Workers' Union, he firmly believes in state intervention in the economy. As minister, he led the charge to impose stricter conditions on Walmart's purchase of Massmart (Game and Makro stores), saying it posed a threat to local industry. At one point, he even suggested that government should cap the salaries of top executives. He has also proposed several economic plans that call for great unity in policy making, but his ideas have now all been superseded by the National Development Plan, the ANC's current new grand plan to fix everything and make the trains run on time *(see p96)*.

One of Patel's great successes is the greater energy of the Competitions Tribunal, which falls under his portfolio. It has become more aggressive, and started to take on cartels in our economy – something to be happy about.

MINISTER OF ENERGY
Ben Martins

Department budget R6.8 billion

Martins first entered Cabinet as Minister of Transport in 2012, but was there for only a year before being transferred to Energy. A former trade unionist, he tried to change the way South Africans behave on the roads, and now he has to convince us to save as much energy as possible. Tricky tasks. But perhaps his trickiest will be ensuring the country has a functioning

Eskom to keep our lights on. Martins has some big decisions to make in the next few years; he'll have to make a call on whether or not we want to focus on nuclear power, and you can expect to see him attracting a few headlines as the fracking of the Karoo becomes more likely.

MINISTER OF HIGHER EDUCATION AND TRAINING
Blade Nzimande – *see p156.*
Department budget **R31.5 billion**

MINISTER OF HOME AFFAIRS
Naledi Pandor
Department budget **R5.3 billion**

Pandor is the woman in charge of your ID. She has a reputation for efficiency and for getting the job done. She is also seen as one of the old guard of government, having headed Education under Mbeki. As a result, she's got the necessary experience to lead a department that comes under intense pressure from time to time.

Pandor spent part of her early life in London, where she picked up a semi-British accent that Julius Malema once memorably described as "fake". When Zuma took over in 2009, she appeared to be relegated to Science and Technology, but worked hard to ensure South Africa won the battle to host the SKA telescope in 2012 *(see p94)*, before being returned to a more influential position at Home Affairs that same year.

She is now in charge of one of the big departments of state, and will look to improve on the good work done by her predecessor, Nkosazana Dlamini-Zuma, who turned around the department after the disaster that was Nosiviwe Mapisa-Nqakula.

GROOTES POWER RATING ™

MINISTER OF HUMAN SETTLEMENTS
Connie September

Department budget R25.3 billion

September is still relatively new to high office, having been appointed to Cabinet in July 2013 (taking over from the vanquished Motlanthe-supporting Tokyo Sexwale).

She has a real rags-to-Cabinet tale, having come, literally, from the floor of a Western Cape textile factory through the union system to become a leader within Cosatu and then a member of parliament. People who knew her in her early years say she always had the demeanour of a leader, but was humble with it. She rose to prominence during several strikes in the textile sector during the late '80s, when striking was still a very dangerous thing to do.

She now has one of the toughest jobs in government. Urbanisation is happening so fast that there is simply no way government can build enough houses fast enough to keep up with the sky-high expectations of the public. Expect her to find it tough going.

MINISTER OF INTERNATIONAL RELATIONS AND COOPERATION
Maite Nkoana-Mashabane

Department budget R5.1 billion

Despite being our ambassador to India, Nkoana-Mashabane was almost unknown outside of political circles before taking over what used to be the Foreign Affairs department in 2009. Coming from Limpopo, where she'd been an MEC, she had the misfortune of being known as the wife of Norman "Sex-pest"

Mashabane. (Mashabane was convicted of sexual harassment while representing South Africa as an ambassador in Indonesia; he died while still fighting the claims against him.)

Nkoana-Mashabane had a rough ride at first, primarily because people expected a well-known political heavy to take her portfolio, usually seen as the most important for any country after Finance. Over time she has gained a reputation for competence and sophistication. She stays mainly out of the domestic limelight, but has managed to strike up relationships with the likes of former US Secretary of State Hilary Clinton.

In the public eye, it has also helped that she is now, physically, half the woman she once was – a rare example of a politician losing weight while in office. Behind the scenes, she clearly has Zuma's ear, and is able to negotiate her way through difficult diplomatic snafus with the confidence that brings.

MINISTER OF LABOUR
Mildred Oliphant
Department budget R2.1 billion

Oliphant is one of those ministers with a hugely important portfolio who is hardly ever seen in public. As the minister supposedly in the firing line for the problems within our labour system, particularly in the mining sector after the Marikana shootings of 2012, she has been particularly quiet.

GROOTES POWER RATING ™

Oliphant is from KwaZulu-Natal, where she rose up the ranks of the provincial ANC. She has also been active within Cosatu. She came into Parliament in the class of '94, and has mainly played roles within parliamentary bodies, while keeping a low profile.

GROOTES POWER RATING ™

POWER 6 MORAL 5

MINISTER OF MINERAL RESOURCES
Susan Shabangu
Department budget R1.2 billion

Shabangu is one of those ministers who has spent almost her entire life in the liberation movement, working from 1980 onwards in various political formations: the Federation of South African Women, the Free Nelson Mandela Committee, Cosatu. She has been in charge of one of the most difficult portfolios since 2009, but she was famous before that for her comments, while deputy at the Safety and Security ministry, that police should "shoot the bastards" – the bastards being criminals. It was also claimed she'd raised her skirt after setting off a metal detector at an airport. She is not someone to mess with under any circumstances.

A notable battle during her time at Mineral Resources involved Julius Malema's campaign to nationalise the mines. It was a difficult balancing act: she couldn't say outright that our mines would never be nationalised because it was still officially up for discussion within the ANC, and she couldn't say they would be nationalised because, well, that would be bad. In the end, she stuck to the line that "nationalisation is not government policy". It worked, mainly because she had the discipline not to deviate from it at all.

Another great challenge for her came, as it did with Oliphant, after the events at Marikana. The actions of the police, both in causing the massacre and in reacting to it, distracted from most of the heat on Shabangu, but the incident hangs over the troubled mining industry like a spectre. Not long after, she attacked mining firms who said they needed to retrench workers, memorably appearing to threaten to revoke Anglo Platinum's mining licences when it laid off 14,000 workers.

While Shabangu speaks in public from time to time, she tends to give the impression of being slightly disengaged from the real challenges within the mining sector, considering how difficult the situation there really is.

MINISTER OF POLICE
Nathi Mthethwa

Department budget R62.5 billion

Mthethwa is seen as one of Zuma's closest allies, having been brought into the Cabinet from – where else? – KwaZulu-Natal. The fact that he was given the police portfolio, and has managed to keep it, is an indication of the trust the president has in him. Not only is it crucial for Zuma to keep control of the police, but reducing crime is currently one of the ANC's biggest priorities – which makes a nice change from times past.

Though crime statistics are notoriously prone to manipulation, it appears that many of the key indicators have dropped significantly in recent years. The murder rate, for one, dropped by 28 percent between 2005 and 2012, according to police figures. But the rape and sexual abuse plague, no matter what the figures say, remains a national tragedy.

Zuma's trust in Mthethwa seems to stem from his time in the ANC underground. He was another involved in Operation Vula, and was also active in the ANC Youth League, from where he worked his way in to the ANC proper. Within the party Mthethwa displayed his loyalty to Zuma by speaking out against Malema when no other ANC leaders would.

On the downside, his time in office has been marred by certain scandals. He is the minister responsible for allowing Richard Mdluli to head up Police Intelligence amid claims he was tapping phones for Zuma. It also appears Mthethwa suspended an investigation into the looting of a Police Intelligence slush fund to protect Mdluli *(see p225)*. Then came claims, which he has denied, that money from that fund was actually used to build a fence around his home.

GROOTES POWER RATING ™

Mthethwa is currently politically powerful because of his relationship with Zuma and his position on both the NEC and NWC. His position in government seems secure, but he has tied himself to his boss.

MINISTER OF PUBLIC ENTERPRISES
Malusi Gigaba
Department budget R1.2 billion

Gigaba is seen as one of the upcoming men of government, with the brightest of futures. He is young – under 40 when appointed to Cabinet – and, it seems, hugely ambitious. He is also the best dresser in Parliament.

Gigaba came up through the ANC's ranks by leading its Youth League. He was elected to that post almost through acclamation after a strange set of events that saw a conference almost dissolve before he was suddenly elected uncontested. While leading the League he was mostly known for his loud criticism of the Springboks, claiming our rugby was racist and needed to transform. Attitude, yes. Julius Malema, no.

On becoming too old to lead the League – yes, this is possible – he entered Parliament, before being made deputy minister at Home Affairs by Mbeki. Apart from an unfortunate incident involving the departmental credit card and flowers for his wife, he seemed to emerge from the experience unscathed. His big break came with the promotion to his current job.

In office Gigaba's ambition has shone forth in claims that he wants to run half the country through the parastatals he controls. But, as the parastatals in question tend to hit the skids from time to time, he is also the person who has to smooth things over in public. He may well get bored of having to justify their massive mistakes. *(See p114.)*

Within the ANC Gigaba is seen as powerful; there was much political chatter in the run-up to Mangaung that he might even win election to the top six. That didn't happen, but he certainly seems to be popular with the right people. That is to say, Jacob Zuma. And because he has youth on his side, he's worth a long-term bet on holding a national leadership position in the future. Some within the KZN ANC even whisper that

GROOTES POWER RATING ™

POWER 7 MORAL 7

he could be part of a plan to keep the Presidency in KZN hands – first Zuma, then Nkosazana Dlamini-Zuma, then…

Gigaba is also the most active minister on Twitter (@Mgigaba), and is happy to join conversations about politics and sport.

MINISTER OF PUBLIC SERVICE AND ADMINISTRATION
Lindiwe Sisulu

Department budget R700 million

When it comes to struggle heritage, it's hard to touch Lindiwe Sisulu. The daughter of ANC legend Walter Sisulu and the sister of National Assembly speaker Max Sisulu, she has been in the corridors of power for many years and in Cabinet since the Mbcki era. She has served as minister in Housing, Intelligence and, under Zuma, Defence – which is where the wheels appeared to come off for a bit.

It emerged, after much baiting from the DA, that she'd been using military planes and helicopters to travel between Gauteng and Cape Town, costing millions. When she was rumbled, she was furious, and she told the DA's David Maynier he was "flea-ridden". If he'd used the same language about her, thermonuclear war would have resulted. But she regained her sense of humour when he presented her with a travel pillow as a present. She gave him a calculator, claiming he'd got his sums wrong.

Sisulu in person can be imperious, and she appears to like to have her own way. She is one of the best-dressed people in Cabinet, and always makes sure she has a snazzy gown for the opening of Parliament.

Her current job is to keep the civil service in line, which basically means dealing with unions. She might wish she had a brigade or two from her time in charge of the army to help her along.

GROOTES POWER RATING ™

MINISTER OF PUBLIC WORKS
Thulas Nxesi

Department budget R8 billion

Nxesi is the man in charge of the stinking mess around the president's home in Nkandla. If you hear that word, his name is unlikely to be too far behind.

Nxesi rose through the political ranks at SADTU, going on to lead a large international teachers' union federation. Eventually he was called by Zuma to come to Cabinet where, on his arrival, he found his department in a complete mess. Because it controls property and resources, Public Works is a department that's easy to loot. Work costs can be inflated, money can go missing – and he has to carry the can. And because Public Works is also responsible for the accommodation of cabinet ministers, it's often in the news for all the wrongs reasons – as when they end up staying in five-star hotels rather than in their official residences.

Nxesi has been very honest about the state of dysfunction within his department. At one point he even told Parliament that his department needed to be taken "into administration", and that he needed people from the Treasury to help him fix it. But the brownie points he gets

GROOTES POWER RATING ™

for his honesty here disappear when it comes to the Nkandla situation. There it appears Nxesi has decided simply to cover his boss's behind, obfuscating and tergiversating rather than letting the truth emerge. Nkandla has hampered Nxesi because it has prevented him from speaking in public often (to avoid the obvious questions).

(See Nkandla, p227.)

MINISTER OF RURAL DEVELOPMENT AND LAND REFORM
Gugile Nkwinti

Department budget R8.9 billion

GROOTES POWER RATING ™

For someone responsible for perhaps the country's most contentious and controversial long-standing issue – land redistribution – Nkwinti has remained virtually silent since his appointment. He also appears to have done very little to speed it up.

This could well be a calculated strategy. By talking up land redistribution, the ANC would only be building up hopes, which would probably then be dashed. As a result, the party needs to control the debate without letting it build up too much steam.

Nkwinti has produced proposals to change land reform policies; however, at twelve pages long they were rather short on detail. He has now started to push for a "valuer-general" who would determine the value of land to be taken from farmers, to be given to those who lost it.

GROOTES POWER RATING ™

MINISTER OF SCIENCE AND TECHNOLOGY
Derek Hanekom

Department budget R5 billion

Hanekom is one of the country's nicest and most honest politicians. He became politically active when he and his wife were thrown off their farm in the late '70s because it was on land being taken for a homeland. He then joined the ANC, served two jail terms for his political activities and went into exile in Zimbabwe.

On his return, Hanekom was part of Mandela's first Cabinet, and famously asked to exchange his fancy ministerial car for an old 4x4.

He seemed able to negotiate with Afrikaner farmers, who were very nervous about the change in government. Though he subsequently left government for a time, he's always been highly respected in the ANC, and he was head of the party's National Disciplinary Committee when it had to deal with Julius Malema in 2011. He took many of the decisions that led to Malema's expulsion.

Hanekom was bumped up from deputy of his department in 2012, and has worked hard to keep up the momentum in what is a traditionally low-profile ministry. If you've actually noticed it in the news in recent years, it is likely only because of its involvement in the bid for the international Square Kilometre Array radio telescope, which will receive foreign funding to the tune of R15 billion or more. In 2012 it was announced that, though split with Australia and other countries, the majority of the project would be coming to South Africa. With major construction work in the Karoo and full operation only due in 2024, Hanekom should have plenty to keep him busy.

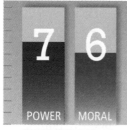

POWER MORAL
GROOTES POWER RATING ™

MINISTER OF SOCIAL DEVELOPMENT
Bathabile Dlamini
Department budget R112 billion

A veteran of Parliament since 1994, Dlamini rose up the ANC's ranks through its Women's League, and was its secretary-general for ten years, until 2008. She was heavily involved in turning the League against Mbeki and towards Zuma in 2007 – so no surprises, then, that she's from KwaZulu-Natal.

While in office she has kept a fairly low profile, despite the fact that she's responsible for the portfolio with the largest budget by a considerable distance (literally off the chart on p72). This is because Social Development is the welfare department. R120 billion has reportedly been allocated for spending on social assistance in the 2014/5 financial year, and with 15 million South Africans – more than 30 percent of the population – benefiting from grants, she's got a lot of people relying on her.

MINISTER OF SPORT AND RECREATION
Fikile Mbalula
Department budget R800 million

Mbalula used to be the young firebrand of our politics. When he was Youth League leader, until 2007, he was the Julius Malema before Julius Malema. At the time, he was a rabid Zuma supporter, long before it became fashionable. And because of his leadership position, he was able to campaign for Zuma in public while most other ANC leaders kept

GROOTES POWER RATING ™

quiet. He was rewarded for this devotion with a deputy position in the Police ministry, before being given the Sport portfolio in 2010. It was tailor-made for him. If there is one thing Mbalula can do, it is lead the cheers of a nation for its sports teams. Despite a well-publicised extra-marital affair in 2011, he's fared as admirably as could be hoped in a department that, in the quota-obsessed past, used to attract rather a lot of negative press.

Interestingly, his pro-Zuma proclivities have changed over time, to the extent that he pushed for his former-hero's removal from office at Mangaung. Since backing the wrong horse there, he has been a shadow of his former self, hardly appearing in public and being very quiet when he does.

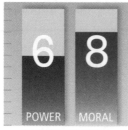

POWER   MORAL

GROOTES POWER RATING ™

MINISTER IN THE PRESIDENCY: NATIONAL PLANNING COMMISSION
Trevor Manuel

Department budget R1 billion

Manuel is one of the longest-serving ministers in post-democratic South Africa, having led the Finance ministry for 13 years under Mandela, Mbeki and Motlanthe. During that time he established an international reputation for competence and prudence, and was known for his ability to control public finances. He also built up the capacity of the national treasury to ensure that our money is properly accounted for. His reputation was such that when he (temporarily) resigned from the post, when Mbeki was recalled in 2008, the Johannesburg Stock Exchange dropped 4 percent in a matter of minutes.

He came to politics young, and was part of the United Democratic Front during the '80s. On the day Nelson Mandela was released, Manuel

The National Development Plan

The NDP, the handiwork of Planning Minister Trevor Manuel, is South Africa's new grand-master, slightly Chinese-style plan that will, over the coming decades, sort out the economy, make sure our children are educated and prepared for the future, and essentially leave the country better off than how we found it.

When Manuel was put in charge of Planning in 2009, no-one really knew what he would get up to. What he did was gather together South Africa's best experts – in everything – and draw up the best way to improve the country. The result is a long, involved project that takes into account everything: where our water will come from, how to best provide electricity, was the person who introduced him to the massive crowd in front of Cape Town's City Hall. He had a bright future ahead.

But Manuel was seen as tied to Thabo Mbeki; when Zuma won at Polokwane his star began to dim a little. In 2009 Zuma put him in charge of Planning, where he has created a well-received National Development Plan. The plan is relatively capitalist for a document coming from an ANC government, and contains several highly controversial suggestions. If it is actually implemented it could see Manuel's influence lasting many decades into the future. *(See sidebar.)*

At the ANC's 2002 Stellenbosch conference, Manuel received the most votes among those on the NEC. Ten years later, by Mangaung in 2012, he chose to no longer make himself available to serve in the NEC, and seemed content to accept a lower-profile posting. This has led to suspicions he may be preparing to leave front-line politics.

Manuel is married to Maria Ramos, who he met when she was his director-general in the Treasury. She is currently the CEO of Absa Bank – which means she earns more than he does.

how judges should be selected, what teachers should do, and so on.

Unsurprisingly, it's controversial. For example, it seems to embrace a youth wage subsidy, which would see employers being subsidised by government for giving people their first job. A great idea. But absolutely hated by Cosatu and the SACP, and thus a very hot potato.

Nevertheless, Zuma himself used the ANC's Mangaung conference to give the NDP his seal of approval, and the conference adopted the plan as official ANC policy. That isn't going to stop its opponents from fighting its implementation, though, and already there are doubts about it being implemented, in whole or in part.

MINISTER IN THE PRESIDENCY: PERFORMANCE MONITORING AND EVALUATION
Collins Chabane

Department budget R1 billion

Chabane, from Limpopo, is seen as one of Zuma's closest allies, which in itself should confer a fair bit of power. Considering his job allows him to monitor and evaluate how other ministers are doing, that should give him even more power. And considering Chabane has made other ministers sign performance contracts, he would seem to have a rather big stick to beat them with and wield his power. And yet it's simply gathering dust somewhere; he doesn't ever seem to use it.

The idea of monitoring performance was supposed to be Zuma's big thing in office. But instead it's become something of a damp squib. Certainly, Chabane has not played a major role in getting anyone fired or even disciplined for non-performance.

In person, Chabane is incredibly friendly. He's the kind of guy who will get you a drink before you realise he's actually a minister, and quite important. He's also well known for his marimba, having once – and I'm really not making this up – played in a marimba band at the Oppikoppi music festival.

MINISTER OF TOURISM
Marthinus van Schalkwyk

Department budget R1.4 billion

Forever doomed to go down in history as the last ever leader of the nasty National Party, Van Schalkwyk has only kept his position in Parliament because he brought the Nats into the ANC. At the time, 2005, the ANC was desperate to keep control of the Western Cape, and this coalition allowed them to do that. As a result, he got a Cabinet post even though he now has no natural power base of his own. This is a bit awkward for him; he sometimes gets invited to the ANC's NEC meetings as an "observer" but without voting or even speaking rights.

However, he's made up for this shortfall by being energetic and competent at whatever he does. He seems to have done very well in his portfolio since 2004, making sure that all the boxes are ticked whenever ticking is necessary. He was previously the Minister of Environmental Affairs and Tourism; the department was split in 2009 when Zuma expanded the Cabinet.

MINISTER OF TRADE AND INDUSTRY
Rob Davies

Department budget R9.1 billion

Davies is from the SACP, and sometimes his communist beliefs show. He's one of the men who tried to impose stricter conditions on the deal that saw Walmart buy Dions and Makro, and has appeared to interfere in business more generally. He is also responsible for trying to force all businesses in the country to register with their local municipalities. If you've ever

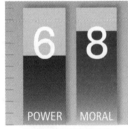

GROOTES POWER RATING ™

spent time in your local council offices, you'll know that's probably the kiss of death for most smaller firms. Under pressure, he withdrew the Bill, but it still left a sour taste in the mouth of those who care for business.

Davies spent part of the 1970s and all of the '80s in exile. He's a very senior member of the SACP and is on its top leadership body – which, despite this being the 21st century, is still called the Politburo.

Up close, Davies can be abrasive, and he tries not to stand for any nonsense. But, unlike many other politicians the world over, if you ask him a question you will get a straight answer – and it won't be based on the identity of the questioner. He's one of those politicians who do actually think before they answer, and tries to give everyone a fair hearing. Don't annoy him, though. He has a sharp tongue and he's not afraid to use it.

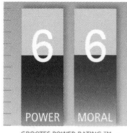

GROOTES POWER RATING ™

MINISTER OF TRANSPORT
Dipuo Peters
Department budget R38.8 billion

Peters is from the Northern Cape, and thus wasn't known to too many people when she came into national government, despite being the province's premier. She came into politics through the lesser-travelled road of the church, joining various Christian organisations before leading several student movements and, through them, joining the UDM.

In four years at the Energy ministry she managed to keep out of the limelight even as the provision of light, as well as its cost, dominated the news. She could argue, though, that Eskom does officially come under Public Works, so there was very little she could do. She only came to the Transport ministry in July 2013, and is likely to have to take a higher profile now as a result.

In person she seems warm and approachable, and she has started to take part in conversations on Twitter (@DipuoPeters). She is also very strong on gender issues, and the empowerment of women generally.

MINISTER OF WATER AND ENVIRONMENTAL AFFAIRS
Edna Molewa

Department budget R13.3 billion

GROOTES POWER RATING ™

Molewa started in politics while teaching, and was involved in the ANC's various underground structures during the 1980s. She played leading roles in several union movements, becoming deputy president of catering union SACCAWU, before playing a role within Cosatu. She became an MP in 1994, before going into provincial politics in the North West and rising to premier of that province in 2004.

In national government she has become more prominent since being appointed to her current department in 2010, largely because of the publicity relating to the recent surge in rhino poaching. She might argue that the fact that South Africa's water systems aren't making the news is indicative of how well they're working at the moment, but many people would disagree with that.

Molewa is also a major power within the ANC Women's League, and is quite happy to argue with anyone who tries to oppose the rights of women.

MINISTER OF WOMEN, CHILDREN AND PEOPLE WITH DISABILITIES
Lulu Xingwana

Department budget R200 million

GROOTES POWER RATING ™

When this ministry was first established in 2009, many people scoffed at it, suggesting it be renamed the "Ministry for Everyone but Men". It's a pity that, with the appointment of Xingwana to this portfolio, the scoffers were proved right.

Xingwana made a real hash of things at Agriculture amid claims she had interfered in the running of the Land Bank and was actually trying to influence various deals. Unfortunately, her reputation for a lack of competence has stayed with her in her new job. Famously, she has stormed out of an "immoral, offensive" exhibition that included images of lesbians; she was accused of spending upwards of R2 million on furniture for her head office; and she was criticised for discriminatory comments directed at Afrikaners in light of the Oscar Pistorius murder case.

From time to time she appears in public to decry the amount of violence against women in this country. But considering our horrendous rape and sexual assault statistics, involving both women and children, she remains far, far too quiet.

A mark in her favour was her public opposition to the Traditional Courts Bill, where she publicly opposed the powerful Minister of Justice Jeff Radebe because she objected to traditional chiefs having certain powers over women. She won out in the end, as she and a coalition of civil society organisations were able to force government to withdraw the proposal. A bit more activity along these lines would be welcome. This is a position crying out for a real gender activist. Imagine Winnie Madikizela-Mandela in this role, and we might start to see a real difference.

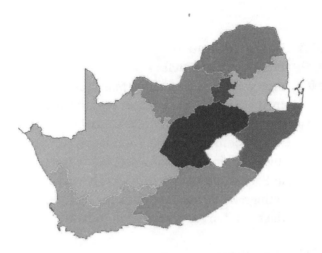

Premiers and provincial leaders

Formally, premiers are elected to their posts by provincial legislatures, with the winning party thus effectively getting to choose the premier. Pretty straightforward. But it is ANC policy for its NEC to decide who the premier will be, and it instructs the legislature in question to vote accordingly. Logic would have it that the provincial leader – as voted by ANC provincial delegates – should end up as the premier, and this is supposed to happen because, well duh, that would make sense, wouldn't it? But it often doesn't, for various political reasons.

In Gauteng for example, the NEC didn't want Paul Mashatile to be premier because he's not a Zuma-ite, and so ordered legislature members to vote for Nomvula Mokonyane. The ANC also doesn't announce who its candidate for provincial premier will be before elections – not the most transparent process.

The Western Cape has the only non-ANC premier, Helen Zille. It, too, likes to mix up the premier and provincial leader. Its legislature voted Zille in after the DA made her its official candidate in that province, while the party leader in the province is Ivan Meyer.

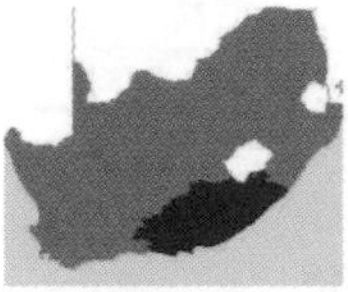

Eastern Cape

Premier **Noxolo Kiviet**

Provincial leader **Phumulo Masualle**

In the Eastern Cape Kiviet appears to concentrate on running the province in government, while Masualle runs the ANC. This used to be the engine room of the ANC, and its biggest province by far, but it's been hit by infighting and major service-delivery problems – in particular around Port Elizabeth, where leaders have reportedly come to blows during meetings. In the meantime, the province remains a disaster and the lives of the poor don't appear to be improving.

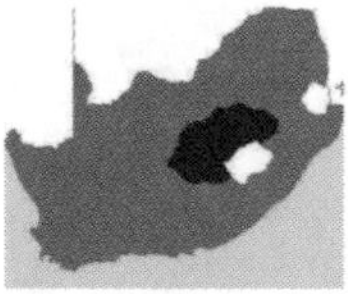

Free State

Premier and provincial leader **Ace Magashule**

Magashule was leader of the Free State ANC for over a decade but Mbeki consistently refused to allow the ANC to appoint him premier. He finally got the nod in 2009, having strongly backed Zuma's Polokwane campaign, and has supported Zuma ever since. He likes his provincial websites to cost at least R40 million.

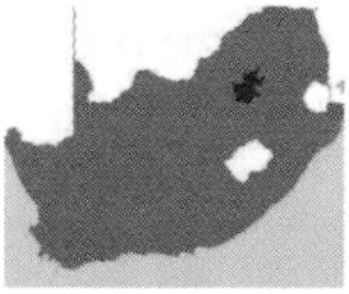

Gauteng

Premier **Nomvula Mokonyane**

Provincial leader **Paul Mashatile**

Mokonyane has been premier since 2009, and is widely regarded as being quick to talk and possibly a little bit slower to act. As mentioned, she is in office but not in power in the province, with Mashatile the leader of the Gauteng ANC. She supported Zuma at Mangaung; he supported Motlanthe.

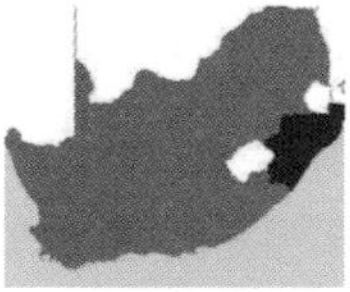

KwaZulu-Natal

Premier and provincial leader **Senzo Mchunu**

Until August 2013, Zweli Mkhize split his time between two jobs: treasurer of the ANC and premier of KwaZulu-

Natal. He played a huge role in making sure the provincial ANC was in lock-step behind Zuma at Mangaung, and is seen as a huge Zuma ally.

Mchunu assumed the premiership after Mkhize's departure, having worked with him as provincial leader to back Zuma.

Limpopo

Premier **Stan Mathabatha** Provincial leader **n/a**

Before his downfall, Julius Malema was more than just leader of the ANC Youth League; it appears he was pretty much running Limpopo. The evidence strongly suggests that, under Cassel Mathale's disastrous premiership, Malema was arranging tenders for people who put money into his bank account in return. Time, and the courts, will tell.

In the meantime, Mathabatha was chosen to be premier by the ANC after five provincial departments were taken over by the national government in 2011. He is expected to bring a clean broom to things, and will have to get the muck of corruption out of the provincial administration. Mathale was the last person elected provincial leader, but was removed from the position by the NEC and is likely to face corruption charges himself at some point.

Mpumalanga

Premier and provincial leader **David Mabuza**

As both premier and provincial ANC leader, Mabuza is the undisputed king of Mpumalanga. And sometimes he acts like it. There have been widespread corruption charges against him from the provincial SACP and Cosatu, and at one point a *Sunday Times* reporter was arrested and thrown in jail, somewhat coincidentally after writing stories about him.

Northern Cape

Premier Sylvia Lucas Provincial leader John Block

Lucas was appointed premier of the Northern Cape because the leader of the ANC in the province, Block, is a man who faces some serious corruption charges. Block has managed to stay in charge of the provincial party despite what seems to be very damning evidence that he has manipulated hospital tenders. It appears that Lucas was put in charge by Block because she's weak and he can control her.

North West

Premier Thandi Modise

Provincial leader Supra Mahumapelo

Modise was the deputy secretary-general of the ANC when she was asked to go and run the province in 2010 because the provincial ANC was so divided it couldn't get anything done. Mahumapelo is currently the provincial chair, but leads a province in such disarray that leaders have been known to break up the meetings of other leaders with sjamboks. Just before Mangaung, shots were fired at one leader. This is also the province that saw its councillors handing over Tlokwe to the DA in 2012, with much resulting consternation at ANC headquarters.

Western Cape

Premier Helen Zille Provincial leader Ivan Meyer

As leader of the DA, Zille's time is obviously split between provincial and national policies. But then Jacob Zuma's time is split between being leader of the ANC and being president of the country, so in a way she has it easy...

The ANC's provincial leader (and Deputy Minister of International Relations) is Marius Fransman, a man who's not shy of a headline.

Chapter Nines

Our constitutional watchdogs; the gamekeepers of government;
useful places for re-deployees

"Chapter Nines" are institutions created under Chapter Nine of the Constitution to keep a check on state power. They are supposed to be part of government while watching over government. To do so, they must be independent, and on paper they are. As the Constitution puts it, they are "state institutions supporting constitutional democracy".

How they run

Chapter Nines receive a budget from government, are led by people chosen by Parliament, and are told to get on with it. In some cases, as with the Public Protector, they have a wide-ranging brief. People can file complaints or they can choose to examine a situation themselves. But the sole purpose of the Independent Electoral Commission is to run elections.

As these are relatively new organisations in South Africa, the work they do tends to reflect the kind of leader they have at the time. In the case of the Public Protector, it was a very weak institution under Lawrence Mushwana, who held the position from 2002 until 2009. When Thuli Madonsela took over things changed dramatically *(see p111)*. The Human Rights Commission (HRC) was very active once upon a time but has quietened down since Mushwana was transferred there. (This may not be a coincidence...) No-one really knows who's led the Commission for the Promotion and Protection of Cultural, Religious and Linguistic Minorities, because it's raised its head just twice – once to complain that the SPCA was racist when condemning Tony Yengeni's spearing of a bull, and once to moan loudly about Zapiro cartoons. They don't like shower-heads. (Don't worry if you haven't heard of the Commission for the Promotion and Protection of Cultural, Religious and Linguistic Minorities. Those who have are themselves a very small minority.)

On a day-to-day basis, Chapter Nines have the capacity to conduct investigations and hold hearings. They are able to ask for evidence, and government bodies have to comply. Thus if they want to investigate, say, the Andries Tatane murder, or the Nkandla scandal, then the ministries involved have to cough up the relevant information. Sometimes those under the spotlight can obfuscate or delay, but in the end the will of the Chapter Nines must be done. It is this that gives them so much power – because, unlike so many other political entities in the country, they can actually access the information they need to thoroughly review a matter.

For obvious reasons, Chapter Nine findings are usually made as public as possible, making it very difficult for them to be ignored. When Madonsela, as the public protector, released her report on the police headquarters leasing scandal in 2011, it indicated that then National

---

South Africa's Chapter Nine institutions are:

- **Public Protector:** effectively the public ombudsman, with power to investigate any government entity.
- **Auditor-General:** reports on the finances of government at all levels; has the power to audit any tax-payer-funded organisation.
- **Independent Electoral Commission (IEC):** runs all elections.
- **Independent Communications Authority of South Africa (Icasa):** regulates electronic comms

Police Commissioner Bheki Cele and Public Works Minister Gwen Mahlangu-Nkabinde were guilty of corruption. Because these findings were public, Zuma was forced into acting; he fired them both. Also on her recommendation, he fired Cooperative Governance Minister Sicelo Shiceka, who was partial to the odd luxury trip at the taxpayer's expense.

How they are played

These organisations have had a tendency to get politicised. Because their senior positions are chosen by Parliament, the ANC ends up doing most of the choosing, and there have been instances of these appointees then supporting certain ANC figures. During the Zuma rape trial, the Commission for Gender Equality (specialising in gender equality, remember) turned a blind eye while his supporters sang "burn this bitch" outside the court. Eventually the SAHRC, guided by more independent-minded leaders, decided to investigate the matter. In the process, it was able to shame the CGE into making it a "joint investigation".

The claim has also been made by the DA that the SAHRC sometimes makes findings against the City of Cape Town that are political. This is where it gets complicated, because it's hard, without having full access to the facts, to say whether some outside toilets are worse than others. The Makhaza case notwithstanding *(see p222)*, it is opposition parties that

(cellphones, landlines, internet, broadcasting) and post office.
- **South African Human Rights Commission (SAHRC):** monitors and investigates human rights violations.
- **Commission for Gender Equality**

(CGE): promotes gender equality through various avenues.
- **Commission for the Promotion and Protection of Cultural, Religious and Linguistic Minorities (CRL Rights Commission):** self-evident.

seem to leverage Chapter Nines most effectively to score political points.

As the independence of these organisations is constitutionally enshrined, the only way for a ruling party to try to make them compliant is to ensure that the people who run them are compliant. It's the usual story. If you want to nobble an organisation, nobble the person in charge. So far this has worked. However, opposition parties have become wiser to this, and are more wary when the appointment of new heads are made and more adept at creating media heat around these appointments.

Two of these Chapter Nine institutions, the Public Protector and the Auditor-General, are seen as more important than the rest, due to the roles they play in guarding against government corruption and maladministration. As a result, the Constitution is very careful to create specific criteria for the people who run them. And, perhaps more importantly, it then makes it very difficult for those people to be removed. For both organisations, there is a lengthy process involved when attempting to remove their heads, climaxing in a vote in the National Assembly, where a two-thirds majority is required. This gives both the Public Protector and the Auditor-General a very free hand in which to operate. Of course the corollary is that if someone unsuitable is put in charge, it's going to be very difficult indeed to get him or her out.

Likely future

Over time, what were supposed to be completely non-partisan bodies have become, slightly inevitably, politicised. They've been used by various parties, and by factions within those parties. As has happened to date, the future of each one will tend to rely on the person who is leading it at that particular time. It seems likely they will grow even more important as ANC dominance wanes slightly and our politics becomes meaner over time, which makes their politicisation even more the pity. These are important organisations that should be left free to play the roles they were intended for – protecting the rights of the people of our country – rather than getting stuck in the political gutter.

Thuli Madonsela

Born: 28 September 1962

The public protector; defender of the weak; student of corruption; one of the strongest independent voices in our democracy

Thuli Madonsela has probably the softest voice of any public official in the southern hemisphere. When meeting her, the first question you ask yourself is, how can someone with one of the loudest voices in our cacophonic democracy be so quiet? How has she managed to not succumb

Timeline

1994/5	2009	2011	2012
Contributes to drafting the final Constitution.	Appointed to head Public Protector.	Gets Cele, Mahlangu-Nkabinde and Shiceka fired.	Starts Nkandla investigation.

to the South African disease of thinking that the louder you shout, the more important you are? In fact, unless you are listening closely, you may find yourself missing what she's saying. And that would be a pity, because she is always worth listening to.

Madonsela has a scholarly background. Before becoming public protector in 2009, she was commissioner of the Law Reform Commission, where her role was to examine old laws and consider new ones that may better serve contemporary South Africa. In doing so, she would have studied reams of paper and thought closely about their outcomes.

Worthy and important, yes. But proper preparation for the post of public protector? Probably not.

And yet Mandonsela has single-handedly revived the office of the Public Protector. Unlike many other people in this book, she realises that the power of words lies not in their volume, but in how you choose them. And she chooses incredibly well. She has a stern belief in her independence and a desire to make sure that complaints are properly investigated and the correct remedies enforced.

By the end of his tenure, Madonsela's predecessor, Lawrence Mushwana, had become the lamest of ducks. To many, it seemed his role was simply to deny complaints against the ANC; the only time he would take action was when he had to decide between different factions within the governing party. When his term was over, he took a massive payment of nearly R7 million, and a week later he was the brand-new chair of the Human Rights Commission. Without even the decency to be slightly embarrassed about it.

Madonsela is different. As mentioned already, she has taken on investigations and released findings that have forced Jacob Zuma to actually fire ministers, as well as a police commissioner. As a result, she has come under tough pressure from sections of Parliament. Her deputy,

Kevin Malunga, has been publicly critical of her, leading to claims from ANC MPs that she is acting unilaterally. She also faced corruption allegations of her own in 2011; conveniently timed to coincide with her investigation into the police headquarters leasing scandal, they turned out, unsurprisingly, to be baseless.

Onward she ploughs, though, safe in the knowledge that a push to remove her from her post would require a two-thirds majority in Parliament. And anyone who knows how difficult it is for the ANC to get all of its MPs in Parliament at once, let alone whip up the necessary support from smaller parties, knows that's just not going to happen.

Likely future

Of course, Madonsela does need to be careful. Even if those in power can't remove her, they can still weaken her. They can fill her office with people she can't trust; they can make public claims that she's autocratic, leading to a lack of public trust. She will need to be wary so that she doesn't find herself still in office but with no respect from the public.

For the moment, Madonsela is one of those people who investigates like a bulldog and punishes through her quiet, well-chosen words. For the good of the country, let's hope she is doing exactly the same thing in five years' time.

Eskom
SANRAL SAA SABC SA Post Office
DENEL Telkom Transnet
ACSA

Parastatals
Or: State-owned enterprises (SOEs)

The state-run drivers of government policy; the nexus of analysis paralysis; the doers of almost nothing; permanent disaster areas

It's hard to find a proper textbook definition of *parastatals* (alternatively, state-owned enterprises or SOEs). South Africa has more than 700 of them, which allows for a fair bit of variety. But in short, they are organisations, businesses or entities that are wholly or partly owned by government, with specific state-oriented mandates. So the SABC is the "public" broadcaster, Transnet runs our railway system, SAA is the nation's airline, Telkom provides us with high-speed internet.

Yes, textbooks can be wrong.

Problems: money and power

In the beginning… parastatals were supposed to be a way of making things function without government having to pay for them. In other words, Telkom would be a semi-private company; it would run our telephone system and make a profit while doing it. A similar process would allow our railways and electricity to pay for themselves via Transnet and Eskom. It's clever; taxpayers aren't lumbered with the cost, and the service actually gets provided. But there seems to be a fatal, chaos-generating flaw within the structure of modern South African parastatals. It goes to the heart of how they're governed, and that wonderful phrase "cadre deployment".

Most parastatals are wholly owned by government; there are no other shareholders. As a result, government gets to appoint the boards of directors of those parastatals, usually through the minister responsible. (Eskom and SAA come under the Public Enterprises Ministry, while others are appointed by Cabinet.) The boards are then supposed to simply get on with the job. They appoint a qualified CEO and other necessary positions, and the organisation then runs itself from there.

Key to the effectiveness of this concept is the idea that the board, once appointed, is fully independent. But this is hardly the case. Never mind the argument that the best possible people should be found to run parastatals; being government-owned, government tends to want them properly "aligned" with government's aims. The logic here is that only someone who has the same type of politics and the same priorities as those in government should be allowed to run such an important organisation. And this is where cadre deployment comes in – when politicians interfere with the key appointments to these institutions.

In time, many parastatals, along with their boards, have become deeply politicised. The SABC is a good example. Possibly the best.

2013 saw major upheaval at the public broadcaster. With its chair of the board, Ben Ngubane, seemingly trying everything in his power to cast the ANC and Jacob Zuma in glowing light, other board members felt they should consider the country and SABC as a whole, and so disagreed with him. In one instance, most of the board wanted to fire Hlaudi Motsoeneng as acting COO, while Ngubane wanted to protect him – because, it appears, that would have been in Zuma's best interests.

Long and complicated story short: the board collapsed and everyone resigned. Quite something, right?

Except that the SABC has been mired in similar crises for the better part of a decade. So, no, the Ngubane meltdown seems to have been just another day at the office. (Read up on Snuki Zikalala's time at the SABC for politicising of the newsroom that would have done Stalin proud.)

Another prime example of political intervention comes in the form of the Siyabonga Gama affair at Transnet. Gama was in charge of Transnet Freight Rail when he was accused of giving a R19-million contract to a security firm run by then Communications Minister Siphiwe Nyanda. He was found guilty of corruption by an internal disciplinary hearing, and it appeared he would be fired. At the same time, the ANC's deployment committee – which does exist; it is a real thing – had decided Gama should be the new CEO of Transnet. Gama's proceedings were put on hold for a bit and then a new board was appointed to Transnet. Next thing, he was reinstated as head of Freight and everything was, we were told, fine and dandy. The ANC, and no doubt Gama himself, were very happy. But it made a complete mockery of the independence of processes.

One of the other unavoidable problems of parastatals is that they deal with so much money and hand out such large contracts that it's just too tempting for politicians to keep their grubby mitts off them. They can't help themselves. Combine this factor with the varying amounts of political power involved, and some parastatals will attract more trouble than others – specifically those with more money and power. This is why the SABC is always in the news; it has both political power through its broadcasts, and large budget through its size, thus there will forever be fights over it.

More problems: incompetence

Possibly the greatest problem that parastatals now face – certainly the one that affects you and me the most – is a direct consequence of the problems above. Because senior appointments are being made according to political motivations rather than aptitude for the job, our most vital parastatals are inevitably getting themselves into difficult positions. There has been a long period during which people who are politically connected, but not necessarily properly skilled, have been placed in top jobs. They coast along for a while, but eventually they start to make mistakes. Next thing you have rolling blackouts and the electricity crisis of 2008.

And so big mistakes are made that cost big money *(see sidebar opposite)*.

At the same time, those who have been passed over either leave or choose to make trouble – and the trouble-makers are becoming more and more problematic. Because it becomes a political lottery when deciding who is appointed to the top jobs, unions in some parastatals have started to campaign for their candidates. When their candidates lose – because another political grouping gets its man appointed – that union starts to actively work against them. This can see workers spying on their bosses, or insane claims being made in a bid to raise tensions. It has become common for senior appointments to be accused of racism or corruption or the like, hoping to simply muddy the waters.

The future of parastatals

There are so many parastatals doing so many different things that it's unlikely there will ever be a wholesale change in the way they're run, except over a long time period. While there has been a "Review of State-owned Entities", its final report appears to have made no hard recommendations about what should be done. It does seem that some parastatals could slowly become government departments over time. At the moment, the issue has effectively been kicked into a touch.

Blackouts, bailouts and payouts: SA parastatals			
PARASTATAL	WHAT THEY DO	IN THE NEWS FOR	INTERESTING STAT
Eskom	National electricity utility	Blackouts. And enormous electricity price hikes since its disastrous 2008	R50 billion. Estimated cost to the economy of 2008 electricity crisis
SAA	National airline	Bailouts. By government to keep the airline running	R16.8 billion. Government bailouts to SAA since 2004
SABC	National broadcaster	Payouts. To executives who leave the broadcaster, usually under a cloud	More than R25 million. Amount paid out in golden handshakes since 2010
Denel	National arms manufacturer	Being the country's best-run SOE	R157 million. Value of Denel's Airbus A400 contract

African National Congress / ANC

Founded: 1912
Slogans: A better life for all; Together we can do more

South Africa's majority party; the guys in charge; the only party that really matters; to some, "the people who will ruin the country"; to most, "our liberators and the voice of the people"

The ANC is an international phenomenon. It is one of the most renowned liberation movements of all time and can produce an enviable roll call of great names from its past: Plaatje, Seme, Luthuli, Tambo, Sisulu, Mandela… Officially the voice of the majority of the land since 1994 – before that it was

Timeline

1914	1944	1952	1961	1990
SANNC travels to UK to petition for rights.	ANC Youth League founded.	Defiance Campaign begins.	Umkhonto we Sizwe established.	ANC unbanned, Mandela released.

the unofficial voice – the party in power has never won less than 62 percent of the national vote.

And yet it is a curious beast, sheltering beneath its broad wings a wide and sometimes contradictory array of thinkers and leaders and wannabe leaders. Having made the transformation from liberation movement to governing party (although it still denies this), it

GROOTES POWER RATING ™

finds itself never far from the headlines, in constant flux and with ever-deepening factional divisions. Will it rule South Africa till the Second Coming, or are there tumultuous and difficult times ahead?

A brief history

The ANC, as anyone who was alive and able to look at billboards in 2012 will know, was formed in Bloemfontein a century before, by a group of representatives of the black elite at the time. They wanted to petition the British authorities to allow them more rights and to give them more freedoms, which they first did in 1914, sending a small group of members to the UK. Even for them, the idea of equal rights or one-person-one-vote would have seemed very radical. The dominant personality here, and later ANC president, was Pixley ka Isaka Seme, and one of his main priorities was to do away with the tribalism that had made it so difficult to unite black people in South Africa against colonial rule. At first the

1994	1998	2001	2007	2008
Wins SA's first democratic elections.	Mbeki elected party president.	Senior ANC members implicated in Arms Deal.	Polokwane conference signals power shift to Zuma.	Mbeki recalled as president of the country.

South African Native National Congress, as it then was, moved slowly. They sent another delegation to the Treaty of Versailles discussions at the end of the First World War to once again petition but, quite predictably, they were once again ignored.

The most notable explosion in the ANC's membership numbers came during the 1950s, once the mechanisms of the new apartheid state started swinging into action. Nelson Mandela, Walter Sisulu and others launched demonstrations and protests against National Party rule as its discriminatory legislation – even more so than before – came into force. People were being classified by colour and, if not white, removed from their communities and dumped in the worst parts of the country; pass laws were introduced to limit their movements; the population was being segregated at every level. With thousands of people being mobilised, the Defiance Campaign turned the ANC into a mass movement.

After Verwoerd's Nats cracked down on this resistance, eventually banning the South African Communist Party and ANC, so the ANC started the armed struggle, again with Mandela in the forefront. There was much moral agonising over this decision, but in the end it was agreed that military targets would be hit, with every effort made to ensure civilians weren't killed. Then Mandela and other ANC leaders were arrested, at Lilliesleaf Farm in Rivonia, where after they went through two Treason Trials before being sentenced to prison on Robben Island. It was at the climax of the second trial that Mandela made his now-historic speech *(see quote, opposite)*.

After Rivonia the ANC went underground, and non-jailed senior members into exile, some to London and many to other parts of Africa. The armed struggle technically continued, but the ANC was forced to focus on campaigning for sanctions against apartheid, building up support around the world. Within South Africa resistance seemed to wither, hitting a nadir in 1967 with the death of its long-standing president, Albert Luthuli. The Nats would have had everyone believe that the ANC didn't even exist. Famously, no photograph of Mandela reached the outside world, and his wife, Winnie, though banned to Brandfort in the Free State for many years, seemed to be a lone voice. While Tambo, Thabo Mbeki and others did their best from abroad, local protest was led by the Black Consciousness Movement and later the United Democratic Front. The Soweto riots of 1976 marked a tragic landmark in the struggle, as black schoolchildren protested new legislation that meant they would be taught in Afrikaans. And then came the turbulent '80s as the townships erupted and the apartheid state entered its death throes.

In 1990 FW de Klerk, having recently succeeded PW Botha, declared a change in policy, unbanning the ANC and releasing Mandela and others from jail. The ANC had won its great battle, and now came the time to govern. With Mandela in charge, it came into office in 1994, and it has remained there ever since. And there are plenty of smart people arguing about how long it will stay there for.

Structure: Branch – Region – Province
To join the ANC you need to be an adult South African, or a spouse or child of one, who has "manifested a clear identification with the South African people and its struggle", or a South African resident who has done the same. At the base of the ANC is the branch, so you contact your local branch, pay your R12 annual membership and you're in.

"During my lifetime I have dedicated myself to this struggle of the African people. I have fought against white domination, and I have fought against black domination. I have cherished the ideal of a democratic and free society in which all persons live together in harmony and with equal opportunities. It is an ideal which I hope to live for and to achieve. But if needs be, it is an ideal for which I am prepared to die." – Nelson Mandela, Rivonia Trial, 1964

Luthuli House

The ANC's headquarters on Sauer Street in the Joburg CBD have changed dramatically over the years. Now named for ANC stalwart Albert Luthuli, the building was known as Shell House when the party first moved in after its unbanning. It was the scene of the 1994 Shell House Massacre, when ANC security guards opened fire on around 20,000 IFP supporters marching on the building. Nineteen people died and eleven were later given amnesty by the TRC for their roles in the incident. In September 2013, the building suffered an arson attack in its reception area, a room often used for press conference, which became famous when it saw the public announcement of Julius Malema's first expulsion from the party.

"Luthuli House" has become a metonym for the ANC and is sometimes used to imply that the ANC's national leadership controls everything, from ANC branch meetings to big government decisions.

Every member of the party has to belong to a branch, which has to have regular meetings to stay "in good standing". Under normal circumstances, branches are expected to have more than 100 members, but there are branches with several thousand members. One in KZN has more than 8,000. (As Gwede Mantashe describes it, when that branch meets it's not a meeting, it's a rally.) The ANC tries to ensure that branches are divided among municipal wards, with each ward having a branch, but if a branch gets too big, it may then split off so that one ward can have several branches.

Branches have a leadership structure, they hold Branch General Meetings and can undertake their own disciplinary hearings. As an example, Atul Gupta was hauled before a disciplinary by the Saxonwold branch after treating Waterkloof Air Force Base as his own personal driveway.

Luthuli House has battled to keep the number of branches stable.

Because each branch is supposed to send one delegate to ANC conferences, in the run-up to elective conferences there tends to be a sudden explosion in the number of branches. As it costs just R12 to join the party, it'll only cost you R1,200 to create your own branch if you want to cook the books... This has become a major problem over the years, and is unlikely to stop being a headache.

All branches belong to geographical regions. Often these regions are not named after their areas, but people, so there's the OR Tambo region in the Eastern Cape, for example. The size of a region can change vastly from place to place. The OR Tambo region is the second biggest in the country – so big that what it decides literally determines what the Eastern Cape ANC will do. (The biggest in the country is inevitably the eThekwini region around Durban.)

The regions fit into the provinces, which then make up the national structure of the ANC. Over time, the provincial leaders within the party have grown to have some serious power in their own right. For example Ace Magashule in the Free State and John Block in the Northern Cape have become almost unstoppable, largely because of their time in office. Block in particular has serious corruption claims against him, and yet is still running the show there.

When it comes to power at this level, size matters. Because the ANC in KwaZulu-Natal has more members, it has more branches, and thus more delegates at elective conferences. This is why Jacob Zuma won so easily at Mangaung. KZN had so many votes that it was literally able to dictate the outcome. The only province that comes close to it in terms of numbers is the Eastern Cape. However it was divided on who to support, and in the end its leaders backed Zuma.

This also means that some provinces are so small they hardly matter. The Northern Cape has very few ANC members, while the Western Cape, despite its concentrated population, also has a relatively small number of members. This means Luthuli House can safely ignore these provinces for the moment.

Voting for leadership

Branches hold Branch General Meetings to elect their leaders, and then send delegates to regional and provincial conferences. These delegates then vote according to the wishes of their branch. In many cases delegates are not told specifically who to vote for, but just to represent the wishes of the branch – so the possibility for candidates to be encouraged to change their minds during the conference itself is pretty high.

Provinces have conferences to elect new leadership usually every three years. These can be very important because those leaders determine who the province will support at the national level. They can also lead to strange circumstances. For example, the National Executive Committee of the ANC appointed Nomvula Mokonyane as premier of Gauteng, but the regional delegates chose Paul Mashatile as provincial leader. While the two do seem to get on amicably enough, there are times when it seems the leadership is actually split.

Every five years, around eighteen months before the country's next national election, the ANC holds a national conference to choose new leadership. Beforehand, the branches and then regions meet and vote on their leadership candidates. About two weeks before the national conference, the provinces hold their Provincial General Meetings, and because they pronounce on who they want when the meetings conclude, it's usually at this point that you are able to work out who will come out trumps at the national conference. The number of delegates from each province is known so it's (usually) simply a case of adding them up to see who will be the next ANC president, and thus president of South Africa.

Policy

ANC policy discussions are hugely important because of the party's dominant role in government. But because the party is now so large, with various factions and agendas, it's almost impossible for it to actually make hard and firm decisions. And then it's even harder to implement them. The Polokwane conference, for instance, saw firm decisions on land redistribution and a Media Appeals Tribunal that have not been implemented. Almost the only decision from the conference that went through was the one to disband the Scorpions.

Inevitably in a party that is so big, policy discussions are managed. There are several commissions, covering health, communications, education, gender transformation and economic transformation. The chairs of these commissions then draw up policy discussion documents, which are widely circulated. Branches are supposed to discuss these documents and tell their delegates what they want to do. Those delegates then go to conference and discuss those issues in the commissions. A commission reaches a decision about, say, nationalisation of the mines, and takes that back to the plenary session, at which everyone at the conference can speak. Then the conference will "pronounce" on a decision.

But that is often only the starting point. Those who oppose a particular policy will often still fight it during the implementation stage. A good example is the ANC's decision to implement a youth wage subsidy, which Cosatu and the SACP have managed to block, at least for the moment.

National Leaders: The top six

From president through to treasurer, the ANC top six are the party's national leaders and the positions everyone talks about.

■ *President, currently Jacob Zuma*

The president is, of course, the boss of the ANC. The guy in charge. But he is usually president of both the party and the country, so while he has the power, he actually spends his time in the Union Buildings and doesn't run the ANC on a day-to-day basis. *(See p57.)*

■ *Deputy president, currently Cyril Ramaphosa*

The deputy president is in the same position. Either the president's closest ally or his archrival, he is usually in government – barring corruption charges or anything like that – and therefore spends most of his time running the country, not his party. *(See p132.)*

- *Secretary-general, currently Gwede Mantashe*
- *Deputy secretary-general, currently Jessie Duarte*

  Unlike the president and vice president, the secretary-general has no governmental position. He's the guy who runs the day-to-day affairs of the ANC. Think of him as the party CEO. With the simple task of making an enormous governing political party operate smoothly, he gets an entire floor at Luthuli House to work from, but he is often in the field dealing with problems that crop up in branches and regions across the country, from Kakamas to Kuruman. While the president is obviously in charge, the secretary-general operates as his enforcer. As a result, this is often seen as the most important job within the ANC, the power position. A good S-G will keep the party growing, and ensure it's in lock-step behind the president. A weak one will allow it to slip, losing control of provinces and regions and thus the whole operation. He has a deputy, usually an enforcer in her own right. *(See p136 and p143.)*

- *National chairperson, currently Baleka Mbete*

  The chair of the party has a deceptively simple job: she runs ANC meetings. So she chairs the National Executive Committee and ensures these meetings go smoothly. Her power comes in the form of deciding who speaks when. Thus as a debate unfolds, if she's a smart operator, she can almost determine how it will play out. *(See p140.)*

- *Treasurer-general, currently Zweli Mkhize*

  As the name suggests, the treasurer-general manages the ANC's money. This is the person responsible for ensuring there's enough money in the pot to campaign for elections. Given that the party reportedly spent almost R200 million on its 2009 campaign, that's a large amount of tom that can go missing. The ANC, already a massive and complex operation, has grown recently, and has accounts that can best be described as opaque. With ongoing controversies involving its investment company Chancellor House, and whether the party really does benefit from Eskom contracts, the treasurer is someone who has to be trusted by the other leaders. But, as Mathews Phosa's recent history shows us, often isn't. *(See p142.)*

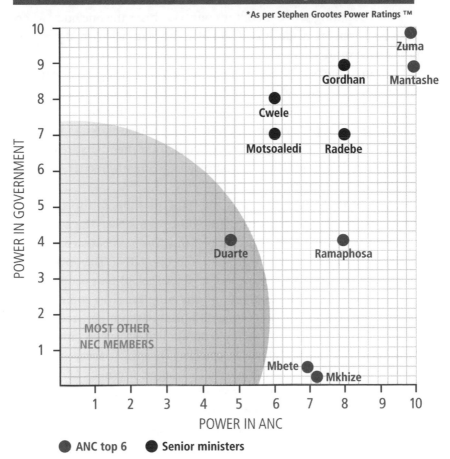

Power within ANC v Power within government*

*As per Stephen Grootes Power Ratings ™

ANC top 6   Senior ministers

The National Executive Committee / NEC

The National Executive Committee is the ANC body we hear most about on our radios and in our newspapers. It's the all-powerful group of 86 people – the ANC top six are the officials, plus 80 additional members – who essentially run the party between national conferences. If you get on the NEC you've officially hit the big time, and have the power to take part in all manner of decisions, from choosing the décor at Luthuli House to, say, firing the sitting president of the country. This is the one body where the big decisions are made. It is, if you like, the place where real power in South Africa resides.

To get on to the NEC you have to be voted on by delegates at national conferences. It's a straight shoot-out: hundreds of people stand, the delegates vote, and those with the most votes get on. But there's a caveat. For the sake of proper gender representation, a formula kicks in after a certain point in the counting to ensure that half the members are women. If you look through the NEC election results, women will often make up the last third of the page.

Because of this electoral system, the NEC is supposed to represent the various groups and constituencies within the ANC. The additional members used to number 60 members, but this was boosted to 80 at Polokwane to make sure it was properly representative. The downside is it's unwieldiness. You can imagine that trying to get 80-plus people, never mind 80-plus politicians, to agree on anything requires some serious manoeuvring. There's a reason Gwede Mantashe is so highly regarded.

The NEC meets regularly, usually around once every two months, but special meetings can be called for certain reasons. At these meetings, leaders of the ANC provinces, the Youth League, Women's League and Veterans' League are invited, and sometimes have speaking rights.

Chaired by Baleka Mbete, the meetings usually last between two and four days, and are marked by impressively tight security. As NEC members walk in, there is a desk laid out with scores of brown A4 envelopes with their names on them. As they pass, they are supposed to submit their cellphones so that they can't leak information as the discussions are happening. That's right, cabinet ministers aren't trusted by their own party, and thus have their phones taken away... It's quite something. In recent years, there have been strong and interesting rumours that the ANC has actually brought jamming equipment to place around the halls of these meetings, because people have been smuggling in their phones anyway. Either way, leaks tend to continue, despite official anger at them. The reason for this is simple really. If you're in the NEC and you're losing an argument, it's tempting to leak details of the argument to the public to try to get public support behind you, which may then swing the argument your way. It's clever. And naughty.

The National Working Committee / NWC

The National Working Committee is a separate smaller committee – the ANC top six plus up to twenty NEC members – which meets more regularly than the NEC to run the party to "carry out decisions and instructions of the NEC". It usually meets every second Monday, and tries to keep an eye on things between NEC meetings. While the NWC is powerful in that it can set certain agendas, it's really at the NEC level that power resides.

The ANC Women's League / ANCWL

As a body, the Women's League's primary job is self-explanatory. It's supposed to help push the cause of gender equality both within the ANC and in the country at large. But its copybook has been quite badly blotted by the fact that it often puts politics ahead of women's rights.

The worst public example of this was during Jacob Zuma's rape trial in 2006, when it refused to criticise his conduct in any way. Though Zuma was ultimately acquitted of the charge, he admitted to having intercourse with someone half his age – the daughter of a (dead) friend – at a time when the League was supposed to be campaigning against inter-generational sex, and his testimony revealed worryingly outdated and patriarchal attitudes to women. Worse still, he made no effort to censure supporters outside the court who demanded vengeance on his accuser and carried sexist banners.

The League's image has not been helped by the fact it has failed to put up female candidates to take on Zuma. At one point before the Mangaung conference, one Mpumalanga League leader, Clara Ndlovu, suggested South Africa "wasn't ready for a female leader". This was rightly condemned as another example of the organisation putting politics before its real mission.

The fact that the League is currently led by Angie Motshekga, one of Zuma's biggest allies, might offer some explanations. But to be fair, the League has started to be more active and more involved in the fight against patriarchy. The stringently enforced 50-percent female quotas on both the NEC and NWC do suggest that it is having some influence on the state of South African politics.

The ANC Youth League / ANCYL

If Julius Malema were still leader of the ANC Youth League, he may well have featured on this book's cover. At the very least, he would have received his own entry. Now that he has been expelled from both the League and the ANC itself, the organisation he used to head up has almost disappeared into political insignificance. It's a pity, because it has a proud and important history.

Formed in the 1940s, with Nelson Mandela and Walter Sisulu among its leading lights, it took on a role of agitating for stronger measures in the fight against apartheid. With the unbanning of the ANC in 1990, it was reformed within South Africa by one Jackie Selebi, and it started to become influential again. In particular, its leader before Polokwane, Fikile Mbalula, was able to turn it into a vehicle to campaign for Zuma. During this time the League became famous for its radical calls for policy change, a trend that escalated after Malema took over during a highly contested conference in Bloemfontein. (You may remember the images on the front pages the next day. Bare bums featured.)

While Malema's media profile rocketed, his management of the League was diabolical. He simply dismissed provincial leaders who disagreed with him, and tried to run the provinces himself. With fewer and fewer proper leadership mechanisms, the League started to hollow out. When Malema was finally given the boot in April 2012, it was taken over by the ANC's NEC on the basis that it didn't have properly elected leadership.

As an indicator of how far it has fallen, in September 2013 the League endured the humiliation of having to make a public apology "to everyone who was insulted and wronged" by its past behaviour. It now has no free will or any real power. This could change in time – a long, long time.

The future of the ANC

The ANC is still assured of victory in the 2014 national elections. The only questions are whether its share of the vote will decline, and how it will react if it does. There are two schools of thought. The first believes a dramatic decline in the vote, to perhaps 58 percent, is inevitable because opposition voices are stronger, and the ANC itself is more divided and having problems delivering services. The second school argues that life has improved immeasurably for most people under ANC rule, and none of those opposition groups can really match the ANC's reach across the country. The safest prediction is probably a decline to a little more than 60 percent, from its current figure of just under 66 percent.

Zuma is expected to stay on as president after the polls, while Cyril Ramaphosa will probably be his deputy. As the president assigns certain duties to the deputy, we will then have a clearer understanding of whether Zuma trusts Ramaphosa from the responsibilities he gives him. If they're meaningful and important, it will be a clear indication that Zuma is anointing Ramaphosa to take over after him. If not, put your money on Nkosazana Dlamini-Zuma.

Meanwhile, the ANC is also facing more and more pressure, both internally and externally. A split in Cosatu is likely to have a major impact on the ANC, as the unions that leave could well form their own party. That said, power is a strong glue, so many people will want to stay in the ANC in some or other form.

**Stephen Grootes
2014 ANC national
election prediction**

61%

Cyril Ramaphosa

Born: 17 November 1952

*Deputy president of the ANC; trade union hero;
negotiator; businessman; the most confident man in the room;
our next president?*

Cyril Ramaphosa is probably the most interesting member of the ANC
top six because of his incredible back story and very tantalising future.

Timeline

1982	1991	1994	1997	2012
General secretary of NUM.	Head of Codesa's negotiation committee.	Elected chair of Constitutional Assembly.	Resigns from ANC, "deployed to business".	Elected deputy president of ANC.

He has been at the forefront of the major trends in our history from the mid '80s and, having taken a backseat from mainstream politics in recent years, is now suddenly one of the front-runners to take over leadership of the ANC from Jacob Zuma in 2017.

GROOTES POWER RATING ™

Past

Ramaphosa, originally from Soweto, became politically active during the '70s while studying to be a lawyer. Imprisoned a couple of times, as tended to happen in those days, he achieved his first major claim to fame during the formation of the National Union of Mineworkers in 1982. At the time, miners were not represented by one comprehensive body and many of them still lived in compounds effectively segregated along the lines of the languages they spoke. The idea of starting the NUM was revolutionary, in that it would bring together all the people working in the country's most crucial industry if it could overcome the tribalism so prevalent on the mines. And that's exactly what it did.

Quite quickly becoming the most formidable trade union in the country, the union gave its leaders huge political power and ultimately formed one of the founding blocks of Cosatu. Such was Ramaphosa's success as general secretary that by the formation of Cosatu in 1985 he gave the keynote address. He became well known for his skills as a negotiator, being able to parlay the power of the NUM into better conditions for his members at a time when black unions were not exactly welcome in the confines of white business.

After the ANC was unbanned, Ramaphosa was elected its secretary-general in 1991. Someone somewhere realised that if they had access to one of the world's best negotiators it would be foolish not to let him loose on the National Party, and so he became the ANC's chief negotiator during the transition period. Let's just say that he and the NP's Roelf Meyer became used to each other.

After 1994 he went to Parliament, and continued his negotiating role in the formation of our current Constitution. It's worth dwelling on for a moment: Ramaphosa was a (or even *the*) key negotiator in the formation of Cosatu, during the Codesa talks to end apartheid, and in the creation of our wonderful Constitution. That's some record.

But somewhere along the line his relationship with Thabo Mbeki hit the rocks big time, most likely because they had competed for the number two spot behind Mandela. Mbeki was the smarter operator in this particular battle, and Ramaphosa left politics in 1997, being memorably "deployed to business". This put him in the driving seat just as one of the biggest economic trends of the last two decades was getting underway, the move towards black economic empowerment (BEE). Through a series of complicated deals, many of them in the mining sector, Ramaphosa became not just well off, but seriously rich. Like, R6.5 billion rich, according to *Forbes* (though estimates vary, of course).

Dress: Used to wear capitalist suits, has now lost the tie.

Body language: Always the most confident man in the room.

Answer to a difficult question: Turns it back on the interviewer with a wonderfully crafted sound byte.

And yet he's always maintained a following, and has been encouraged to get back into the political ring for many years. It seems his return to front-line – but behind-the-scenes – politics came in 2008, when he was, it has been said, the loudest of many voices within the NEC calling for Mbeki to be recalled during the famous meeting that led to Mbeki's resignation as president.

Present

In early 2012 Ramaphosa was on the disciplinary committee that ensured Julius Malema's downfall from political glory, a move that would have endeared him to many South Africans. But later that year he was caught up in the Marikana controversy, when it emerged he'd put pressure on government to take firm action against those striking at the Lonmin mine. He was a director of Lonmin at the time, and representatives for the miners have tried to claim he was partially responsible for the shootings that followed.

That didn't seem to matter to ANC members, however, because by the end of December he'd been voted in as deputy president of the party, replacing Kgalema Motlanthe, the first time he'd held a top-six position in twelve years. This was a calculated move by Zuma, who realised he needed to balance his ticket with someone who came from the ANC's urban base and understood how business works.

Ramaphosa has been relatively quiet within this post, and has been careful not to be seen to be upstaging Zuma at any time. However, the fact that he's returned to public politics, while clearly living a comfortable life away from it, seems to indicate that he has the hunger to go all the way. Otherwise, why would he bother?

In person, Ramaphosa has what you would call X-factor; he is that rare person who brings a room to a halt when he walks into it. At the same time, he is quite able to stand in a corridor and deal with the kind of attention only a pack of political hacks can provide, which is a sign of his confidence and his sheer ability to deal with questions on the hop. It certainly differentiates him from many other politicians.

Likely future

This is perhaps one of the most disputed questions in South African politics: where will Cyril Ramaphosa end up? It seems more than likely he'll become deputy president of the country after the 2014 elections, because that's how the system works. After that we'll quickly find out how much Zuma trusts him by seeing how many duties he is entrusted with. And after that? Well, the position of ANC leader will be his to lose; he is now the front-runner unless a really strong candidate emerges from somewhere – and the person he needs to watch closely is Nkosazana Dlamini-Zuma *(see p146)*.

Gwede Mantashe

Born: 21 June 1955

Secretary-general of the ANC; architect of the Zuma tsunami; the ANC's organiser, fixer and enforcer supreme; with Zuma, the most powerful political unit in the country

To become the holder of the most important office within the ANC, barring president, you have to have two things in spades. Brains obviously. But the other is patience: the ability to wait for your enemy to make a

Timeline

1998	2007	2007	2008
Elected general secretary of NUM.	Elected chair of SACP.	Elected ANC secretary-general.	Announced recall of Mbeki.

mistake and hang himself. Mantashe has plenty of both. Which makes him very, very successful at what he does – even if the political pressures in the job sometimes make him sound a little dense at times while he tries to balance contradictory constituencies.

Past

Mantashe is another of those ANC cadres who came up through the union movement. Specifically, he is a product of that leadership production organisation, the National Union of Mineworkers.

After growing up in the Eastern Cape, Mantashe went to work on the mines. He's spoken with anger about the time he was fired by a mine boss and, without his consent, put on a train back to the Eastern Cape within two hours. It's an illustrative story, as it would doubtless have been one of the experiences that brought him to the liberation movements.

He became chair of the NUM in the Witbank Region in 1982, rising to the position of national organiser in 1988. After 1994 he continued his rise through the ranks of the union, while also becoming a local government councillor in Boksburg. He likes to tell of how the old whites-only council made sure its last act was to vote through the Freedom of the City for one Andries Treurnicht, the man who had tried to force Afrikaans down the throats of black teenagers in 1976, a move that eventually ignited the Soweto Uprising.

Mantashe was elected NUM general secretary in 1998, and held the position for eight years. By 2006 he had his eyes on bigger and better things, and he was key in fermenting the Zuma tsunami that swept all before it the following year.

"The ANC at 101 years is healthy and strong, is alive, is intact, is bold"
– Mantashe, after disbanding the ANCYL leadership in March 2013

Present

Once in office, Mantashe's first big job was to control the fallout left by Polokwane. Principally, he had to ensure that the Mbeki-ists were kept happy. This was made more difficult after Mbeki's recall in September 2008, when several of his loyal cabinet ministers resigned with him. His real challenge came with the subsequent formation of Cope. It was probably mostly due to Mantashe's patience, and his very real ability to win through the sheer force of argument, that Cope did not gain any more senior leaders from the ANC.

As soon as the Cope fiasco was over, he then had to deal with another dilemma, in the shape of Julius Malema. This Mantashe handled extremely carefully. He let Malema do his worst, and simply gave him enough rope to hang himself.

By this stage it was clear that Mantashe and Zuma were acting as one political unit, and Mantashe came to be seen as perhaps the most powerful man in the country, more so than his boss in certain instances. (It could be argued that he has as much power as Zuma, but wields it more effectively.) This is partly because he appears in public regularly and likes to take part in political debates. He's not afraid of anyone and has the sheer confidence to take abuse on the chin. At one point during the Malema dispute he was invited to an ANC Youth League conference, simply so Malema's supporters could sing rude songs about him. Instead of ducking it, Mantashe pitched up, took a beret from a delegate's head, placed it on his own, and started leading the song himself. There are not many politicians with that kind of confidence.

In some ways Mantashe himself has personified the internal conflicts of the Tripartite Alliance. For four years he was both secretary-general of the ANC and chair of the SACP, which had him acting in contradictory ways at times, depending on which particular hat he was wearing. However, he seems to be fully trusted by both organisations, and thus was able to get away with it.

One of Mantashe's prime assets is his wicked sense of humour, which he uses to defuse difficult situations. He's quite happy to rip off journalists, and will be quick to appreciate the joke if it's then turned on him. (So long as it's done respectfully.) When Jackson Mthembu was caught driving while drunk, Mantashe appeared with him the next week and took the mickey out of him before anyone else could do it, calling him "Jackshon Mthembu" for the entire day. It worked wonderfully, in that it defused the situation and was a public admission that Mthembu had been wrong. *(See p145.)*

During the height of the drama over the "Kill the Boer" songs, Mantashe had to announce that the ANC would join Malema in defending his right to sing them. Mindful of the fact that a man in his position defending these songs could be quite scary to certain South Africans, he, together with Mthembu, stood up and sang *Die Stem* in Afrikaans to proclaim his love for all South African music. He then started a long conversation about the problems at fly-half for the Springboks. As a way of reassuring people, it was sheer genius.

Mantashe is unapologetic about his politics. He wants a much fairer state, one in which black people are able to succeed as easily as white people. And, being true to his time in the SACP, he's not shy about wanting government intervention in the economy. He is also incredibly well read, and will happily quote all the major economic texts at people with whom he disagrees.

On the negative side, the role Mantashe played in elevating Zuma to power, and the closeness of their relationship, has led to some of Zuma's bad press rubbing off on him. For one, he has been accused of behaving in a less than perfect fashion when it comes to defending

How to address him: "Good morning, S-G."

How you know he's coming: He whistles. Usually, the more stressed the situation, the louder it is as he approaches a press conference.

Favourite expression: "That's what you think. From where I sit…"

his boss. The Constitutional Court found that the Free State ANC was wrong to stop Zuma's enemies from attending their meetings, a move that almost threatened the Mangaung conference. This was Mantashe's responsibility, and it could be claimed he misbehaved deliberately here for political reasons. Mantashe has also accused judges of being "counter-revolutionaries" in their treatment of Zuma, in a way that really raised temperatures at the time, and led to questions as to whether the ANC believed it was above the law, and what it might do should certain rulings go against it.

Possible future

Mantashe is in the ANC pound seats at the moment, and he seems to control the party as well as any one person can. He may well have his eye on government office now, but having been Zuma's secretary-general it will be difficult for someone else to trust him. Then again, he could simply make a play for the top job himself...

Baleka Mbete

Born: 24 September 1949
National chairperson of the ANC; scandal
courter; declining political veteran

Baleka Mbete has had a reputation for courting controversy in the past, but has stayed out of the limelight in recent years. As ANC chair, she wields considerable political power at the moment, working full-time at Luthuli House and controlling party meetings.

Mbete came to the liberation movements during apartheid, and was forced into exile, living in several African cities during the 1970s and '80s. On her return, she rose to prominence in the ANC Women's League, then as deputy speaker of the National Assembly from 1996. After the 2004 elections she was promoted to speaker and chaired debates in Parliament.

By then she had already been caught up in various tricky situations. In 1997 it emerged that she had received her driver's licence improperly. While never charged with wrongdoing, her defence that she "didn't have time" to stand in queues did not leave a good impression. She

GROOTES POWER RATING ™

was also one of the MPs found to have misused their travel allowances in the Travelgate affair. She quickly repaid all the money that was involved in that case.

Perhaps the sharpest criticism of Mbete came for the way she managed Parliament – with something of a debate-stifling hand. She threw a DA MP out of the National Assembly after he demanded to know whether then Minister of Health Manto Tshabalala-Msimang was guilty of theft, having been accused of stealing while a nurse in Botswana. She was also one of the ANC MPs who carried Tony Yengeni on their shoulders to Pollsmoor Prison after he was found guilty of fraud.

In 2007 Mbete was elected to the post of ANC chair, partly on the Zuma ticket, though she remained in government. When Mbeki was recalled in 2008, she was then elevated to the post of deputy president of the country, assuming Motlanthe's position as he took Mbeki's. There was speculation that she may retain it when Zuma assumed the top spot after the 2009 elections, but that wasn't to be. In fact, she left government altogether, and was deployed to Luthuli House full-time, where she remains.

Likely future

Despite rumours that Mbete may have had enough of politics, she was re-elected as ANC chair in 2012. It seems this is the last stretch for her, though. She has been in politics for a long time, and can look back with pride on much of her career.

Zweli Mkhize

Born: 2 February 1956
Treasurer-general of the ANC; Zuma supporter;
the man who controls the ANC's purse strings;
2014 elections financier

Zweli Mkhize has been one of Zuma's strongest supporters over the last few years, and has been partially responsible for making sure that KwaZulu-Natal is fully behind the president. In return, Mkhize was made premier of the province in 2009 and then became ANC treasurer on Zuma's ticket in 2012. Though this is technically a full-time post, the ANC was reluctant to relieve him of his provincial duties right away, only doing so in August 2013 when he resigned as premier.

A medical doctor, Mkhize is a no-nonsense kind of guy, someone who wants to make things happen quickly and likes to get stuck in. When starting a circumcision campaign in KZN, he got out his surgical smocks and did a couple himself, just to get the ball rolling. In press conferences, he's the sort of person who answers questions directly and honestly.

Mkhize has not been very vocal in his new role, but he is likely to start finding his feet and becoming louder as time goes on. One of his main priorities will be to find the money for the ANC's 2014 election campaign, a daunting task. No matter what he does, he will face questions from all sorts of people about where the money actually comes from and whether or not he can be trusted to handle it.

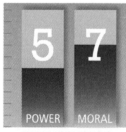

GROOTES POWER RATING ™

Likely future

Mkhize has moved from the provinces to sit at the top table within the ANC, in the trusted position of treasurer. Even though he is seen as a Zuma man, he can expect a national job in government in due course and he may well be in the top tier for some time to come.

Jessie Duarte

Born: 19 September 1953
Deputy secretary-general of the ANC; fierce but
fair fighter with a proud party history

If you've seen the Morgan Freeman film *Invictus*, in which Freeman plays Nelson Mandela, you may have wondered who the youngish woman depicted as his assistant was. Who played such a crucial role at such a crucial time? The answer would be Jessie Yasmin Duarte, someone who has been an integral part of the ANC for so long that her blood flows black, green and gold.

Having campaigned against apartheid back in the day, Duarte first came to public attention in the '90s as the person always with Mandela. She later gained public notoriety when, as MEC for Safety and Security in Gauteng, she was accused of trying to cover up the fact that she didn't have a driver's licence and had delayed reporting an accident she'd been involved in. At the time, everyone was still warm and fuzzy about the ANC, and she would have been one of the first to experience the press turning against her in the form of a very South African type of media outcry, with our complicated dynamic of revolutionary government and entrenched capitalist interests in newspapers. Eventually she had to leave office, only to return to the centre of another media frenzy when Mbeki appointed her as ambassador to Mozambique.

For a while Duarte lay low, but after Polokwane it was clear her star was rising. She was appointed spokeswoman for the ANC, what must be considered one of the most pressured jobs in the country (*see next entry*). It requires poise, self-control and the ability to strategise on the hop. Add the facts that Jacob Zuma had just been elected ANC leader and that Julius Malema appeared on the scene not long after, and you have a recipe for elevated blood pressure.

It was a tough time for the ANC because so much of the media simply didn't trust Zuma, but Duarte, as the public face of the party, was able to appear rational and keep her cool. She was available and managed to control the message while remaining open to criticism. If you asked her to come represent the party in front of a hostile audience, she would grab the opportunity to try to change minds, happy to keep talking until she convinced them of her point.

The stresses, however, eventually appeared to tell, and she was recorded insulting a *Sunday Times* journalist. She then gave a well-known BBC presenter similar treatment on live radio.

In an indication of her closeness to Zuma, Duarte then went to the Presidency to run his office. She appeared to battle in government, clashing with his long-time political aide Lakela Kaunda. Eventually she left, in a bit of a huff, to "pursue other interests". But her relationship with Zuma meant she wasn't going to stay quiet for long. Added to the fact that she is similarly close to Gwede Mantashe, and had worked under him as party spokesperson, it was clear the Luthuli House hierarchy trusted her. By the middle of 2012 she was angling for a top spot within the ANC, and such is her reputation within the party that no-one ran against her when she was nominated for the position of deputy secretary-general.

Duarte is known as a tough nut. She is tiny, but absolutely not afraid of anything. It's funny now to think of her as someone's PA. When meeting her it's hard not to be struck by her obvious intelligence and quick wit. And she can be incredibly gracious when she wants to be. Just stay on her good side.

Likely future

GROOTES POWER RATING ™

As deputy secretary-general of the ANC, Duarte has risen far; there really are only a handful of more important posts in South African politics. A further step up the ladder seems unlikely due to her closeness to Zuma, so it seems she could lose out once he goes. In other words, this may be the peak of her political career.

Jackson Mthembu

Born: 5 June 1958
ANC spokesperson; man at the top table; memorable
phrase-maker; drunk driver

Jackson Mthembu has one of the busiest phones on the planet. As a politician who is suddenly the public face of the ANC, life is tough. And busy. Especially when you didn't really have a huge amount of media experience beforehand. But he has developed quickly on the job.

Mthembu is friendly, a person who is genuinely interested in trying to understand other people. But he's also incredibly fierce when defending the ANC, and will happily jump into any fight. This can get him into hot water, and there have been times when he's spoken before thinking.

But nothing beats the time, in March 2010, when he drove down a bus lane in Cape Town, in morning rush-hour traffic, without bothering to sober up first. In the DA-controlled Western Cape, *nogal*. He was arrested and thrown in a cell, but that didn't stop him from taking calls from the press (about Julius Malema) and trying to do interviews. Eventually Gwede Mantashe arrived to bail him out, while Tony Yengeni, in one of those unforgettable moments of political imagery, went to get a bucket of KFC. You really couldn't make it up. (Mthembu pled guilty, paid a huge fine and got himself back to Joburg as quickly as possible.)

It's important to understand his position within the ANC. He was elected onto the National Executive Committee at Polokwane, then onto the National Working Committee. He was re-elected to both posts at Mangaung. It was the NEC that first asked him to be a full-time employee at Luthuli House, as ANC spokesman. This means he is a political appointment and has the mandate to speak publicly about any aspect of ANC policy. In case you're wondering, his boss is the guy who also bailed him out of jail.

GROOTES POWER RATING ™

Mthembu got involved in politics while still young. He began in Witbank, before ending up in the Mpumalanga provincial government. He rose to become MEC for Public Roads and Transport for a couple of years, before becoming the speaker in that province's Provincial Legislature. A major mover behind the scenes during the run-up to Polokwane, Mthembu crested the Zuma tsunami to win his current post. He is very much part of the Zuma camp, and worked actively to support him during the run-up to Mangaung.

He's well known for his habit of creating phrases, while writing ANC media statements, that sometimes need a little decoding, and he always enjoys finding new ways to insult opposing political parties.

Likely future

Mthembu will be a key element in the ANC's election campaign, and will possibly hope for promotion into national government after 2014. He's been very loyal to Zuma, so may well hope for his reward sooner rather than later. But he does need to watch his mouth – and his drinking. If he makes a mistake, it could be a howler, and of a national magnitude.

Nkosazana Dlamini-Zuma
Born: 27 January 1949
Chairperson of the African Union Commission;
our woman in Addis Ababa; the saviour of
Home Affairs; ANC legend; our next president?

Nkosazana Dlamini-Zuma is one of those rare people who seem able to fix whichever problems are presented to them. Home Affairs was a disaster when she took it over in 2009. Back then a visit to your local office, no doubt a brooding den of doom and dismay, was enough to induce palpitations; entire days off work would have to be scheduled.

Now it's a place where you're greeted by semi-smiling officials, efficiently assisted, and then you emerge back into the sunlight with your passport safely in hand. (Pretty much.) She is also hugely versatile, most notably in her ability to straddle the political divide between Thabo Mbeki and Jacob Zuma in a way no-one else has really been able to do.

GROOTES POWER RATING ™

Dlamini-Zuma joined the ANC during the early '70s while a student. In 1976 she went into exile in the UK, where she completed her medical degree at the University of Bristol. She then moved to Swaziland, which was something of a base for the ANC at the time, with a nicely porous border into apartheid South Africa. While no-one will talk about it on the record, it seems it was there that she met Jacob Zuma. They married and went on to have four children.

Dlamini-Zuma was one of the ANC heavy hitters by the time negotiations started in the early '90s, and became Health minister under Nelson Mandela. In one of the first post-apartheid scandals, she was forced to take some of the rap for *Sarafina II*, a disastrous play supposedly about Aids that cost her department millions. But any bad press she suffered in the department quickly paled when compared to her successor, Manto Tshabalala-Msimang.

By 1999 Dlamini-Zuma had divorced Zuma and become one of Mbeki's favourites. He loved the international stage, and he absolutely trusted her, posting her to Foreign Affairs, where she stayed for a decade.

At Polokwane, that critical moment for the ANC and South Africa, and many ANC politicians, she quite magically appeared to be on both the Zuma and Mbeki tickets – as chairperson on the former's and deputy president on the latter's. This was a huge vote of confidence from both men, but she seemed to go with Mbeki out of loyalty, eventually ending up outside the ANC's top six.

Zuma quickly forgave her, and she was put in charge of Home Affairs, where she made miracles happen. (In 2011 it received its first clean audit in sixteen years.) Then the ANC decided she should be put forward as South Africa's candidate for chair of the African Union Commission, an obvious contender with ten years of diplomatic experience behind her. She was elected to the position in July 2012, in the process becoming one of the most powerful women in Africa. It's a role that has several benefits. Most obviously, it elevates her profile as a competent politician and gives her plenty of high-level networking experience across the continent. But, perhaps more interestingly, it also keeps her away from domestic politics, and its quarrels and scandals. Her current position does, however, limit her influence within South Africa; if and when she returns to Cabinet (or better) her power rating will rocket.

Likely future

With her impressive credentials and an excellent governing record untainted by recent scandal, there are strong suspicions that Dlamini-Zuma is positioning herself to take over from Zuma if he steps down as ANC leader in 2017. For him, it could well be the safe option, as he would likely trust her not to reinstitute those pesky corruption charges against him. Her main challenger for now is clearly Cyril Ramaphosa, so the final decision may well be up to the political machine that Zuma has built within the ANC.

South African
Communist Party / SACP

Founded: 1921

The "clever boys" of the Tripartite Alliance; the original
rooi gevaar; an organisation with a glorious history behind it
– in danger of an inglorious future ahead; Zuma supporter
at all costs – including its glorious history

The South African Communist Party tends to make the South African middle classes see Red. History has it, they argue, that Eastern Europe, Russia and even China had to suffer great swathes of Orwellian tragedy before the defects of communism were proven and renounced, so why does this disastrous theory still retain its ungodly place at the forefront of our politics as one third of the Tripartite Alliance? What are we, North Korea?

Timeline

1922	1950	1990	1993	2005
Rand Rebellion.	Banned.	Unbanned.	Chris Hani assassinated.	Aligns with Zuma.

The Rand Rebellion

In December 1921 a strike by white mineworkers, in response to lowered wages and the promotion of non-whites to skilled positions, turned violent and rebellious. The newly formed Communist Party played a conflicted part in the chaos, railing against the class injustices but opposing the racial element. In March 1922 strikers who had taken Fordsburg, Brakpan and Benoni were met with artillery, air bombardment and 20,000 troops; more than 200 were killed, including several communist leaders. It was something of a forerunner to Marikana 90 years later, and Jan Smuts lost the following election partly as a result.

It's an overwrought question for a number of reasons, but mostly because these days the SACP has become known more for its support of President Jacob Zuma than for any of the principles it used to hold dear. It clearly retains some support, however, and those who claim it has a "glorious" history are certainly not wrong.

You wouldn't think it to look at some of its policy pronouncements now, but the SACP has for long periods kept the ANC on the straight and narrow. It is in fact the SACP that forced the ANC to become multiracial in the first place, for which every South African can be thankful. And when the final history of South Africa is written, the SACP's banner will likely be more prominent than it may seem at the moment – because the party has played a crucial role at crucial times in our past.

The glorious past

Formed as the Communist Party of South Africa under the leadership of William Andrews in 1921 – just four years after Vladimir Lenin's rise to prominence in Mother Russia – it played a prominent role in the Rand Rebellion of 1922. In other words, it's the only political party that can lay claim to driving a South African government to dropping bombs from planes on its own people.

One of the slogans from that time, "Workers of the World Unite and Fight for a White South Africa", makes the point that the strike wasn't just about the money. But the communists chose to become a multiracial political organisation, and they were becoming a force by 1928.

Think about that for a moment. 1928. A time when almost all white South Africans would refuse to shake hands with a black man, never mind fighting for equal rights for all people (well, all *men* really, but *people* sounded better).

The party flexed its muscles with a massive miners' strike in 1946, when 100,000 workers refused to go underground (an event to put some of the mining issues of the last few years in perspective). Its dominant figure at the time was JB Marks, and in some ways this was the golden age of the party. It was able to ensure its councillors were elected, and that its members represented some of the "native seats" in the parliamentary system of the time.

It even had a sense of humour (which appears to have gone missing these days), as when MP Sam Kahn took it upon himself to read *The Communist Manifesto* in Parliament, to ensure it was kept forever in the records of Hansard. This was a work that was banned several years later, so this would have been the height of daring for the time, the 1940s' equivalent of painting an image of a naked president on your garden wall, perhaps.

By 1950 these efforts had led to it being banned – long before the ANC and others suffered similar fates. And, unlike the ANC, it even got to have the banning Act named for it: the "Suppression of Communism Act" was the formal legal instrument.

It was during this time that the SACP started the push to ensure the movement against apartheid was multiracial. At the time the ANC was still black, while a variety of other organisations represented different races. The SACP was the one group that had been multiracial for years, and so played a pioneering role. Its efforts bore fruit in 1955 in the form of the Freedom Charter, which opens with the phrase "South Africa belongs to all who live in it, black and white". Fast-forward four decades to the introduction of the Constitution itself, which draws on the Charter, and we see that it is has evolved directly from the SACP's early philosophies.

In the 1960s and '70s, with many of its leaders underground or in exile, the influence of the party grew due to the support the ANC was receiving from communist countries. The likes of Joe Slovo and Ruth First rose through the ranks and began to take the party into a new era. Already close, the links with the ANC grew even closer, and people like Essop Pahad chose to belong to both organisations, while Thabo Mbeki was a regular contributor, under a pseudonym, to *African Communist* magazine.

In 1990 the SACP was unbanned, along with the ANC and other liberation organisations. It celebrated the fact with a huge rally in Soweto, although it seemed to run the risk of being lost in the public imagination behind the ANC. But its importance within the liberation fraternity was highlighted by the fact that Nelson Mandela insisted on having Slovo as part of his negotiating team – despite FW de Klerk initially refusing to "sit opposite a table with that man". The ill Slovo played an important role, nudging things along when and where he could. We'll never be able to quantify the importance of a white man with an ordinary "white South African accent" breaking down the image of the *rooi gevaar* and helping to allay the middle-class fears that were rife at the time.

It was in fact the relevance and importance of the SACP that led to the most difficult moment in the transition to democracy: when its leader, Chris Hani, was assassinated outside his Boksburg house in April 1993 it brought the country to the brink of civil war. Despite his relative youth, Hani was seen as perhaps the most important liberation leader after Mandela, and he was possibly a step ahead of Mbeki (and Ramaphosa) in the race for deputy president – a clear demonstration of the SACP's power at the time.

By then, the ANC had sold the SACP and Cosatu on the idea of a formal alliance, so they would not contest elections against each other. It seemed a sound strategic decision, but was one that would lead to a long period of frustration for the SACP, and ultimately to its fervent support for Jacob Zuma today.

The problems started in 1996 when Minister of Finance Trevor Manuel, with Mbeki steering things from behind, implemented the Growth, Employment and Redistribution Programme, otherwise known as GEAR – and today referred to by the SACP as the "1996 Class Project", a derisive term for what it saw as a horribly capitalist economic policy. To be fair, a "capitalist agenda" that allowed whites to keep their ill-gotten wealth and moved away from redistribution was always going to be a hard sell to a communist party.

Having supported the ANC, effectively handing it the 1994 elections on a plate, the SACP never forgot their subsequent Mbeki-backed humiliation. When the time came, a decade later, to defenestrate Mbeki, the party took the plunge by backing Zuma to the hilt. While Julius Malema liked to claim it was he who pushed Zuma to the top, it was actually the SACP who did far more. It mobilised people, ensured he got opportunities to speak and campaigned for him everywhere.

On one level it worked – certain SACP leaders were moved into positions of influence in government – but the SACP's familiar problem remains: South Africa's current economic policy has little chance of turning us into a communist state.

The less glorious present
Or: Why are they *sooo* grumpy?

The SACP was very pleased with itself after Polokwane. It claimed responsibility for Zuma's victory and seemed confident things would change. But, like communists everywhere, they were wrong. South Africa is not a communist

What to do at an SACP rally: Rail against the "white racist Helen Zille", sing *Umshini wami*, wear red.

What *not* to do at an SACP rally: Wear a shirt with Julius Malema's face on it. The commies can't stand him.

country. And it doesn't look like becoming one. In fact, it doesn't look a jot closer to communism than it did in 1994. And even on the big-policy issues within government, such as the youth wage subsidy or labour brokers, the ANC simply ignores the SACP when it feels like it.

Unsurprisingly, this has driven the SACP mad. But it has no options.

Blade Nzimande has tied himself to Zuma. This means that everything Zuma does, the SACP supports by default. When the e-tolls furore hit the Alliance in 2011, after government plans to toll Gauteng roads between Johannesburg and Pretoria were announced, the official SACP view was that the toll roads should go ahead but there should be an investigation into how the contracts were awarded – which is a simply illogical stance for a notionally communist organisation to hold when you consider that tolling those roads makes life more expensive for the poor. Problem is, the SACP can't for a moment think of doing anything that will weaken Zuma.

A further irony to add to their pickle: the SACP sees itself as the "clever boys" of the Alliance, with their role to provide the intellectual underpinning of ANC policy – a role that the ANC under Zuma has not really appreciated...

A future without glory?
Nzimande has been general secretary (commie-speak for leader) since 1998. It's hard to see him taking a radical change in direction, and it's equally hard to see who could take over from him. But if the SACP continues to simply follow Zuma blindly it could find itself becoming irrelevant very quickly. One bleak vision of its future is that it somehow muddles through for a while with the current leadership, before eventually disappearing in obscurity.

A brighter vision – for people who believe in communism, that is (or, at least, the balance it brings to the force) – is that it radically changes path, becomes more critical and gains more legitimacy in the view of the public. Or even that it simply wakes up and walks out of the Alliance.

Considering the party has more members now than at any time in its history – *ever* – it still has plenty of potential clout, and the call for it to go it alone is a viable one. But should it? Well, in a way, yes. Technically, it's the party of the "working class", so that's who it should be representing. In the real world, though, there isn't a chance. It simply doesn't have the machinery, the apparatus or the political skill to contest an election.

We're not alone...
De facto communist states:*

1 China **2** Cuba **3** Laos **4** North Korea **5** Vietnam

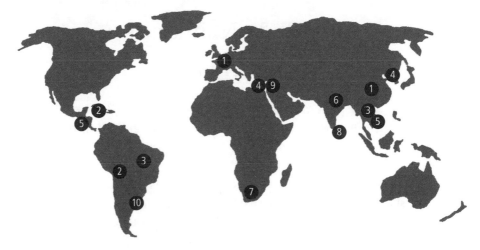

States with communist parties within their ruling coalitions:

1 Belarus   **5** El Salvador   **9** Syria

2 Bolivia   **6** Nepal   **10** Uruguay

3 Brazil   **7** South Africa

4 Cyprus   **8** Sri Lanka

*Traditional communist principles are not fully followed in any of these states; all except North Korea have implemented major economic reforms to move their economies to the free market.

Blade Nzimande

Born: 14 April 1958

SACP general secretary; minister of Higher Education and Training; vertically challenged, bad-tempered Stalinist commie with real rags-to-bourgeois back story

Bonginkosi Nzimande can look back on his life achievements with satisfaction. He grew up in a shack, and in the midst of the bad old days of apartheid managed to obtain a Masters degree in Psychology. If that was all he'd done, it would be impressive. But then he got involved in politics.

Timeline

1976	1998	2006	2009
Attends University of Zululand.	SACP general secretary.	Clashes publicly with Mbeki.	Minister of Higher Education.

Unlike many other people in these pages, Nzimande didn't go to jail for his beliefs, but he did take part in student politics and protests. He was one of those who believed in educating the youth, ensuring their minds were free. So he formed study groups and held seminars to discuss Marxist theory. It might sound very academic, but would have been quite daring at

GROOTES POWER RATING ™

the time. Remember, white activists spent years in jail just for possessing *The Communist Manifesto*; he was actively teaching it.

After liberation, and the deaths of Chris Hani and Joe Slovo, Nzimande shot up the ranks of the SACP, becoming general secretary in 1998. By the time he was re-elected for yet another term in 2012, he'd been in this post for fourteen years; he could well occupy it for a total of nineteen years. But his incumbency has come at a cost. Even before going into government in 2009, he seemed to have become partial to the delights of the bourgeois lifestyle – Doppio Zero is his preferred restaurant, while his wife, Phumelele Ntombela-Nzimande, rose to a top position at the SABC, accruing a top salary along the way.

In the run-up to Polokwane, Nzimande started to really shine, and it was clear that he was becoming more powerful within the ANC because of his relationship with Zuma. He now seemed to be in a position to influence big decisions. It then helped that Zuma offered him the post of Higher Education minister, which tapped into Nzimande's main non-political interest (if you can call it that), education.

But his dual role has been a complete disaster for the SACP. It makes it near impossible for Nzimande to plausibly criticise government when he has been part of the decision-making process leading to the policy that he would normally object to. So the party remains hamstrung, unable to publicly question the ANC.

A comparison of the roles played by Nzimande for the SACP and Zwelinzima Vavi for Cosatu since 2009 – when the former assumed his

R100

price of Nzimande's
first car, in 1981

R1 110 570

price of Nzimande's
most recent car, in
2009 (yes, he's a
communist)

**How to
address him:**
"Comrade Minister."

Quotable quote:
"If there is one
serious threat to
our democracy, it
is a media that is
accountable to itself."

government role, while the latter remained outside government – reveals a noticeable difference in the way they act in the public domain. His sex scandal problems in 2013 aside, Vavi has clearly been more prominent in protecting Cosatu's interests.

Despite the apparent closeness of the Tripartite Alliance, this new status quo is quite a blow to the SACP because it has always thrived on the role of critiquing policy; all of a sudden it has very little to offer. Except, of course, for cheerleading displays whenever Zuma is around. Which leads to the inevitable question: why, from a policy point of view, does the SACP still exist?

And then there are the cars.

Nzimande's first drive was a Volvo. It cost him R100 in 1981. Clearly, when one is a government minister, one should get an upgrade. Or two in his case. So, Comrade Reader, the leader of the South African Communist Party was happy for government to invest the people's money in not one, but two BMWs. For the conveyance of our esteemed Comrade Minister.

Has this helped him to get from A to B? Yes. Has it improved his political legitimacy? No.

Likely future

Nzimande has tied himself to Zuma's coattails so closely that it's hard to imagine him staying on when Zuma goes. He once fancied himself as deputy president, but that seems unlikely now. Especially if the person after Zuma is not a close ally. But he'll probably keep the cars for a while.

Jeremy Cronin

Born: 12 September 1949
SACP activist; deputy minister of Public Works;
poet, academic and contributor to our political
language; regte egte kommunis; perhaps the last
honest man in the Alliance (?)

Jeremy Cronin is a politician who thinks before he speaks. And he is then always honest. That makes him an endangered species.

He's proven his bravery in two major ways. The first: he went to jail for political activities during apartheid. (Can you imagine being white, with white wardens, and going to jail for anti-apartheid activities?)

The second: he spoke up against Thabo Mbeki in 2002 when no-one else would. He told the nation we had to guard against "the Zanufication of the ANC" in what was, in typically clever fashion, a comment that hit Mbeki hard, twice. Firstly, it suggested the ANC was corrupt. Secondly, it showed that following the example of Zanu-PF, which Mbeki appeared to support, was probably bad news.

Cronin is also one of those politicians who will say something, get in trouble for it, and then when you ask him to say it again while he speaks into your voice recorder he'll shrug, sigh and say something along the lines of "okay, one should be consistent and honest" – and then simply repeat his controversial pronouncement.

He also has what is known as a really big hinterland; in other words, he has plenty of interests outside of politics. The first of course is poetry, which appears to have followed naturally from his first academic love, philosophy (in which he received a Masters degree in France).

Cronin grew up in Cape Town (and has retained the accent), and entered politics

GROOTES POWER RATING ™

through the Radical Student Society, before joining the SACP. He was arrested in 1976 and tried on charges of creating propaganda and having dealings with both the SACP and the ANC, both of which were banned at the time. He pled guilty to both charges. Tragically, while serving his seven-year stretch, his wife died of a brain tumour. His first book of poetry, *Inside*, was published after his release.

After the 2009 elections Cronin followed SACP General Secretary Blade Nzimande into both the ANC's National Executive Committee and government, becoming first deputy minister of Transport and then, for his sins, deputy minister of Public Works. The first saw him having to defend e-tolls and the Gautrain, which he had previously opposed; the second is even worse. Imagine being an honest man who happens to be deputy minister in the department overseeing the upgrades to President Jacob Zuma's Nkandla residence… Not an easy position for him.

In government Cronin has been his usual honest self, and remains approachable and fun. He is also one of the most prolific writers in our political scene, albeit prone to rather a lot of Marxist language. He delivers political lecturers regularly which, while they may seem tedious from the outside, are considered pearls of Marxist logic.

Congress of South African Trade Unions / Cosatu

Founded: 1985
Motto: An injury to one is an injury to all

Trade union federation; divided unifier of the working classes; frustrated member of the Tripartite Alliance; organisation at the crossroads of great power – and complete humiliation

Cosatu's main reason for existence is to unify the working class; to make sure that everyone in a job in South Africa is unified in the quest for better wages, better quality of life and political change. Ironic, isn't it? Considering Cosatu itself is now split, almost down the middle, on several major issues. But when it is unified and firing on all cylinders,

Timeline

1990	1996	2005	2007	2013
Joins Tripartite Alliance.	Clashes with ANC over GEAR.	Aligns with Zuma.	Longest public servant strike.	Vavi sex scandal emerges.

Cosatu is the one organisation able to bring the country to a halt with literally 24 hours' notice. And it is also the only organisation capable of getting over a million workers out on the streets and then keeping them there for up to a week.

No other organisation can do that, and that fact alone gives Cosatu incredible power.

An impressive history

Cosatu was formed in December 1985, after the state of emergency had been imposed by PW Botha. Just its creation was a momentous event. It was the joining together of several trade unions in a way South Africa had never seen before, and was the culmination of a very long process. In many sectors several unions first had to merge to form a single union that then went on to help form Cosatu. Two of the main movers behind this were Jay Naidoo and Cyril Ramaphosa, who realised at the time that if all the workers belonged to one unified organisation they would be that much more powerful, and thus able to negotiate better deals from white employers.

At the time, this also led to another major change in union politics. Up until this point many sectors had different unions. Some unions simply represented workers in attempting to secure better wages and working conditions. But others felt that this was merely part of the greater political struggle, and to really improve the lives of their members they were obliged to actively help the ANC and the United Democratic Front fight apartheid. Once Cosatu was formed, there was no more doubt; fighting for workers also meant fighting apartheid.

When the ANC and SACP were unbanned in 1990, Cosatu formally joined them to form the Tripartite Alliance, and in so doing provided much-needed support and organisation for the ANC during election campaigns. With highly organised representation and influence all over the country, Cosatu played a huge role in mobilising voters to support the ANC at the polls.

The gathering storm

Despite Cosatu's close relationship with the ANC, some long-running tensions have developed over the years. Much of the animosity has its roots in the adoption of the 1996 Growth, Employment and Redistribution (GEAR) macroeconomic strategy, which, like the SACP, Cosatu saw as "neo-liberal" and way too capitalist. They felt betrayed by Trevor Manuel and Thabo Mbeki, its architects and promoters. From that point, Cosatu's relationship with Mbeki remained strained, and it was further weakened by opposition to his policies on Aids and Zimbabwe.

These strains were part of the reason Cosatu decided fairly early on to support Jacob Zuma in the run-up to Polokwane. It felt that he was the man who would shift economic policy to the left, and introduce more state intervention. That wasn't to be. Less than a year after Zuma took over the government, Cosatu was publicly declaring its disappointment with him, demanding more economic change. With Zwelinzima Vavi, as ever, leading the charge, Zuma took notice and made some effort to bring Cosatu back on board. *Some* effort.

One of the major reasons why this type of tension between Cosatu and the ANC is never going to ease is that their economic programmes are so different. The ANC pushes for a mixed economy where capitalism plays a big role. It wants to grow the economy by encouraging entrepreneurs. Cosatu (tragically) is much more Marxist. It wants government to control the "commanding heights of the economy". Even worse, it wants to ban private hospitals and schools, and ensure that everyone shares the same prosperity. And by "prosperity" we mean "misery" – because it is all completely unworkable, of course. But that's never stopped a unionist.

Cosatu's power on some issues seems to be almost negligible. Despite years of trying, it hasn't managed to push the ANC to the left or check the party's corruption or even (yet) stop the e-tolling system in Gauteng.

On labour issues, though, it remains the voice that is heard. It has managed to force the ANC to accept several changes to labour laws to do with labour brokers and removing the requirement of ballots before strikes. These are big victories for workers, and will lead to more strikes, strengthening their hand in negotiations. It also means that employers are simply less likely to hire more workers because they don't want strikes. And thus unemployment will rise.

A divided future

Cosatu is facing major issues at the moment in the aftermath of claims that Vavi sexually abused a younger Cosatu employee. While this may look like a split about Vavi, it's actually a split about Zuma. Those who started the campaign to remove Vavi are strong Zuma supporters; those who wanted him to stay don't support Zuma. The real issue is whether Cosatu's support for Zuma should trump its desire to improve the lot of the working class and make their lives better.

If Cosatu doesn't split over this issue in the short term, the chances are it will in the longer term anyway. And the split would be hugely messy; not just a case of some unions staying in Cosatu and others leaving. Unions themselves would split, and it's likely some sort of rival radically left union federation would emerge. This would also see unions fighting for members in different sectors of the economy, with the real possibility of violent confrontations.

All in all, Cosatu's main job is to unify the working class. If it can't do that, it's nothing.

Acronym madness!

There are 21 trade unions affiliated to Cosatu, and the resulting smorgasbord of acronyms is a real mind-bender for anyone slightly intimidated by the complexities of South African politics. From clothing and textile workers to musicians to football players to metalworkers to farm labourers to miners, it gets rather confusing. POPCRU and SATAWU, you may know, but what about FAWU, SASAWU and CEPPWAWU?* Relax. This is why Cosatu exists – for now, at least. If there are two unions under the federation's umbrella that you should know about, then it's the National

Union of Mineworkers (NUM) and the National Union of Metalworkers of South Africa (NUMSA).

The National Union of Mineworkers / NUM
Founded: 1982
The founder of and largest trade union within Cosatu; the wounded king of the union jungle, in danger of losing its crown

What do Gwede Mantashe, Kgalema Motlanthe and Cyril Ramaphosa all have in common? They were all, at one time or another, leaders of the National Union of Mineworkers. If nothing else convinces you of the NUM's importance, that should. Then there's the fact that it's the biggest union in Africa. Or how about the fact it was the organisation that ended what was probably the greatest problem on the mines in the 1980s, "tribalism"? Or that it was a key player in internal opposition to apartheid during the bad old days.

As mining once dominated our economy, so to an extent, did the NUM dominate parts of our politics. Ramaphosa, one of the union's founders in 1982, was key to its early success. It quickly grew, and was able to coordinate negotiations and union activities in the mining sector. By 1985 it was already so strong and well organised that it was able to be the midwife to Cosatu, which then coordinated workers' activities in other sectors. This success catapulted Ramaphosa to the position of ANC chief negotiator at Codesa, which in turn helped to entrench the union's influence.

But recent times have been unkind on the NUM.

As the union has grown, so some of its aims have become less easy to discern. At the same time, some of its top officials appear to have gone to sleep. Essentially, they have become middle class, and thus that old enemy of the working class: bourgeois. So you have workers underground being represented by people sitting in air-conditioned offices above ground.

As a result, the breakaway Association of Mining and Construction Union (AMCU) has started to organise among more poorly paid miners. AMCU itself was formed out of the NUM when its current president, Joseph Mathunjwa, was thrown out of the NUM by Mantashe after a fight between them. The tension between the two unions was one of the causes of the Marikana shootings in 2012.

Political views that matter

Because the NUM has been around for so long and it understands business; it invests all over the place, has swanky headquarters in the Johannesburg CBD, not too far from the Rand Club, and sends around a thousand children of mineworkers to tertiary education institutions through a bursary scheme. As a result, it tends to play a slight handbrake role on the more radical members of the ANC and the Alliance. When Julius Malema managed to elevate the mine-nationalisation argument to front-page news, the NUM strongly opposed him, aware of the damage nationalisation would cause to the industry.

Major problems

The NUM tends to be more understanding of capitalism than other unions, but it faces strong opposition over economic policy from organisations such as NUMSA, and could soon be outvoted in Cosatu debates. Dealing with the threat from its political left, the union now has to work out how to contain demands for it to be more radical. At the same time, prices for platinum (and other metals) have dropped along with international demand (for which we can blame the Europeans and their slow economy); this means the NUM cannot simply ask for higher wages in an attempt to outdo AMCU. Tough times lie ahead.

Likely future

Mining is not as important as it was, and thus the NUM isn't either. But its legacy in our politics will linger for some time, as people like Ramaphosa and Mantashe apply the lessons they learnt in the NUM to politics in the ANC.

The National Union of Metalworkers of South Africa / NUMSA

Founded: 1987
South Africa's second largest trade union;
the radical left of the union movement;
Vavi's biggest supporters

There's something about making BMWs and Mercedes-Benzes that must make you a militant Lefty – because the people who spend their lives hammering the metal plating that clads virtually all the left-hand-drive German sedans on the planet subscribe to the kind of politics that make Karl Marx look right wing. Even their current leader, Irwin (pronounced "Ivan") Jim drives a top-of-the-range Merc himself, while calling for major redistribution. Ask him how government control will grow the economy and you're unlikely to get much of an answer. Meanwhile, all NUMSA members contribute 1 percent of their wages as union fees.

NUMSA was created out of a merger of several metalworkers' unions in 1987. There had been some turmoil within those unions as to whether they should exist just to help workers on the shop floor or actually become political organisations that fought apartheid. NUMSA was created very much to help with the political fight. As the National Party government was trying to entice the international car industry to the Eastern Cape, particularly Volkswagen, BMW and Mercedes-Benz, so the union grew.

NUMSA now has more than 230,000 members, which makes it the

second biggest Cosatu affiliate, after the NUM. Almost all of its members wear blue overalls to work, and many live and work in the Eastern Cape, particularly around Port Elizabeth and East London. It sees itself as a radical counter-weight to the giant of the NUM within Cosatu, and sometimes criticises the NUM in coded form, suggesting it's gone soft. Jim is one of the most outspoken union leaders and often sounds like an older Julius Malema. When the DA organised a march on Cosatu House in 2012, it was Jim who was the first union leader to threaten violence against the DA. He is also one of the strongest and most vocal supporters of Cosatu's general secretary Zwelinzima Vavi, providing staunch support when Vavi is under attack, as when Cosatu suspended him in August 2013.

Political views that matter – if you're incredibly, unbelievably left wing

NUMSA's political outlook is fairly easily grasped: nationalise everything. And they really do mean everything. Farms, banks, Telkom, big firms – like, everything. These are the people who want to make sure private schools are banned, that everyone goes to the same hospital, that there are no rich people. No surprises, then, that they are the Hard Left of the Cosatu grouping – because it's not just about the Commanding Heights of the Economy; it's about *everything*.

Likely future

NUMSA has been making threatening noises about leaving Cosatu. Its leaders are certainly pushing for that. If that happens, the union could either start to organise in other sectors as well, and become a federation in itself, or be the major player in the creation of another federation, playing the role that NUM did during the formation of Cosatu in the 1980s. Either way, it's going to be a very important organisation to watch for the next few years

Zwelinzima Vavi

Born: 20 December 1962

General secretary of Cosatu; formally incorruptible union leader; the ANC's loudest Alliance critic; the man most loved/hated by the middle classes, with the power to bring the country to a halt

Zwelinzima Vavi is a man of stature. Not just by virtue of his six-foot-four height, but by his history in staying in one of the most difficult offices in our country, with huge amounts of power – and yet staying, for a long time, completely clean.

Timeline

1983	1999	2010	2013
Becomes involved in the UDF.	Elected general secretary of Cosatu.	ANC threatens to charge Vavi with ill discipline.	Suspended after rape accusations emerge.

GROOTES POWER RATING ™

As general secretary of Cosatu since 1999 (taking over from Mbhazima Shilowa, who has been spectacularly quiet throughout the rest of this book), he has been the almost undisputed leader of 2.2 million people. And he remained unsullied until late 2013, when he admitted to having sex with a younger Cosatu worker. He was suspended, in a fight that pitted Cosatu affiliate against Cosatu affiliate.

Vavi's real power is that he is so popular with ordinary union members. They have ensured that he is re-elected time and time again, because they like what he stands for. To be blunt, what this country has always needed is a six-foot-four man who is part of the ANC, but completely outside it as well. And that was what he has achieved at Cosatu.

If Vavi had had a good start as a child, it's likely he would have been a player on the international stage by now. Instead, his first job, before he was even a teenager, was as a farm labourer. That would be illegal now, but was the way of life for so many people in his situation. Eventually he headed to the mines, becoming a clerk (in the uranium division, *nogal*). At the same time, he was part of the United Democratic Front, fighting apartheid from inside the country. He rose through the ranks at the National Union of Mineworkers before becoming a provincial secretary of Cosatu in the then Western Transvaal. And then on to national office.

If Thabo Mbeki and Jacob Zuma have one thing in common, it's probably their moments of frustration with Vavi. When Mbeki was at his prime, it was Vavi who told him where to get off on Zimbabwe and Aids. It was Vavi who coined the phrase, as the Shaik trial appeared to be ending Zuma's political aspirations for good, that this man was a "tsunami" who could not be stopped.

And then, after his man had won at Polokwane, it was Vavi, representing Cosatu, who first voiced unhappiness with him and his cronies. Memorably, he declared, "We're headed for a predator state where a powerful, corrupt and demagogic elite of political hyenas are increasingly using the state to get rich." Zuma's free ride was over. Which would have come as quite a shock to him.

It was Vavi again who, in 2011, engineered a situation in which Zuma walked into a Cosatu conference in the cavernous Gallagher Estate conference hall and was met with a silence so cold a polar bear would have longed for global warming. It was an effective political message from him: shape up or ship out.

Such is Vavi's power that Zuma listened. Within months he'd got rid of Cosatu's hated enemy, Julius Malema, and started to act on the issues the union federation was complaining about. Unsurprisingly, Vavi didn't stop there, continuing with his campaigns against both e-tolls and the Protection of State Information Bill. And, despite accumulating an ever-growing number of Zuma-affiliated enemies, no-one would have expected him to stop there either...

Except for the matter of the affair that came to light in July 2013, along with rape allegations and extortion counter-allegations.

Possible future

Vavi was formally suspended by the Central Executive Committee of Cosatu in August 2013. With pro- and anti-Zuma factions pitted against each other, several unions disputed that decision. It is a political conflict that could well be the seeds of Cosatu's destruction. Vavi would seem likely to survive a vote by ordinary Cosatu members, if one were held, rather than a late-night meeting in a smoke-filled room filled with union leaders.

Should Vavi want to, he may decide to create his own union movement, or even his own political party. People who know him well suggest he really has what it takes to create something new from the ground up. But it will be a long hard slog, and there's no proof yet that that is what he actually wants to do. In the lead-up to the 2014 national elections, this will be a story to watch.

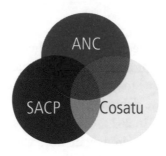

The Tripartite Alliance
Or: Why some really clever people can make themselves sound really stupid

Founded: 1990

The group of organisations that effectively run the country through the ANC; a fractious and ephemeral entity; the non-answer to our biggest political question

Rather as it sounds, the Tripartite Alliance is a formal alliance between the ANC, the SACP and Cosatu. They are three distinct groups with independent memberships and constitutions, and they work together to run the country. Once upon a time the group included the South African National Civics Organisation, but SANCO is now as disorganised as the Johannesburg Billing Department, and is thus ignored.

There are two main interpretations of the role of the Alliance.

Timeline

1912	1921	1985	1990
ANC founded.	SACP founded.	Cosatu founded.	Alliance formalised.

First interpretation

It's a very good thing. People in the organisations that make up the Alliance will tell you its inherent strength lies in the fact that it ensures that all groups of people are represented in government. So the "Left" is represented through the SACP, workers' unions through Cosatu, and what some still call "the people" through the ANC. On this argument the mere existence of the Alliance means there is peace in the land, miners never go on strike and everyone's son will captain the Springboks.

Second interpretation

It's a very bad thing.

The Alliance's enemies – essentially any group interested in politics that is not in the Alliance – claim this is a dastardly trick by the ANC to ensure it will never face competition from a "black" political party. Their argument (and by "their", I do mean Helen Zille and co) runs as follows.

The ANC has co-opted Cosatu and the SACP into their party. By doing this, workers and "the Left" have been bought off so that they will never go it alone. Thus, there will never be true democracy. P.S. The ANC is evil.

If you've ever stood around a burning piece of meat and heard someone lamenting into their beer the fact that Zwelinzima Vavi has never run for office independently, it's because of this argument.

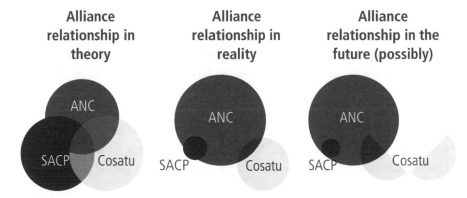

| Alliance relationship in theory | Alliance relationship in reality | Alliance relationship in the future (possibly) |

The Truth

It's a little bit of both.

It's certainly true that in many decolonised African countries the first opposition parties to challenge the liberation organisations have come from the unions. Think Zimbabwe. Robert Mugabe's Zanu-PF ruled almost unchallenged for years, until the Movement for Democratic Change came along. And that sprung from the Zimbabwean Congress of Trade Unions, which could be seen as Zimbabwe's Cosatu. So the ANC is, if you look at it cynically (and we're dealing with politicians here), benefiting from the fact that the people who would naturally challenge it are within its tent. And yet, up until the Marikana shootings in 2012, it did seem as if the Alliance's mechanisms worked pretty well. There was no revolution that saw the rich with their backs against the wall – partly because of the Alliance.

The main drawback to this strategy is that the various factions within the Alliance now have to live with people who they would normally oppose. Which is how you sometimes found Vavi and Julius Malema, who couldn't stand each other, sitting on the same stage together.

In essence the question the ANC had to ask itself was this: would they prefer to have people outside the tent pissing in, or people inside the tent pissing out? They've removed the potties from their tent and placed them outside, for now.

How it works

While there are regular meetings and workshops and indabas and endless prognostications in very expensive conference centres, the Tripartite Alliance is actually quite an informal arrangement. The SACP and Cosatu are presumed to want the same things as the ANC: a better life for all, and particularly for the "previously disadvantaged". So, they're supposed to work towards that in their different ways: the ANC through government, Cosatu through fighting for the rights of the working class, and the SACP through raging impotently against capitalism (or something).

When election time comes, the ANC will include on its party lists some members from Cosatu and the SACP to ensure they go through to Parliament. Once they become MPs, the ANC then appoints them to Cabinet and other positions so they have a chance to exercise power. This is how you end up with a communist, the very effective and efficient Rob Davies, as Trade and Industry minister, and Cosatu's Ebrahim Patel as Economic Development minister.

It also means that when the leader of the ANC has to form his Cabinet, he has to balance the various members of the Alliance. So in 2009 Zuma decided to put his own man at Treasury, Pravin Gordhan, but because the SACP and Cosatu wanted real leftward movement in the economy, he put Patel at Economic Development – while ensuring that Gordhan had more power. This is the problem for the SACP and Cosatu: when they do end up in Parliament, it's in positions of less power and esteem. But with equally powerful BMWs.

Their other problem is even more difficult to handle. As cosy as this arrangement may sound, it means that Cosatu and SACP members who go into government have to toe the ANC's line when it comes to voting. So, while Cosatu is totally *against* e-tolling and the Protection of State Information Bill, its members in Parliament have to vote according to the ANC's decision; in other words, *for* both contentious issues. Even worse, they then have to defend that vote in public. And if you're wondering about the moral hypocrisy of such a position, well, then just think about Blade Nzimande cruising around in his BMW 750i…

There are other, what might be termed "political", methods of managing the Alliance. In 2007 Gwede Mantashe was elected chair of the SACP. Later that year he was also elected secretary-general of the ANC. So for five years he has been in all the meetings that mattered in both organisations, and has unsurprisingly played a coordinating role. Or, if you prefer, he's kept the SACP in line by making sure it didn't ever criticise the ANC or Jacob Zuma. And it doesn't.

At the same time, both Cosatu and the SACP nominate some of their leaders to be voted into the ANC's National Executive Committee. The idea is that they can then speak on behalf of their organisations in NEC meetings. And as we know, it's the ANC's NEC that really runs the country.

The end result
Complete confusion and chaos at every turn.

If you were brought up to believe that politics always made sense, then observing the Tripartite Alliance in action should disabuse you of that particular notion in good time. As the current setup stands, it's common to have someone raging against a piece of legislation outside Parliament, and then voting for it in Parliament. Or Gwede Mantashe could back one economic policy as ANC secretary-general, and another as SACP chair.

Likely future.
Or: The biggest question mark in South African politics
The only question that matters: *If, or when, will the Alliance break up?*

Smart-arse answer: When the interests of the various parties within it are sufficiently diverse.

Longer, more complex answer: It depends on how long they can all stand each other. If Zwelinzima Vavi stays on as Cosatu general secretary, and Zuma stays on as ANC leader, the two are likely to keep fighting in their politically coded ways. Eventually one will lose his temper good and proper (it'll be Vavi; Zuma never loses his temper) and break away from the Alliance. They've come close a few times.

In 2010 Vavi really got under the skin of the ANC when he spoke at a conference of NGOs. For the ANC, this was proof he was taking Cosatu away from them and towards something else. He was going to be the South African Tsvangirai, moving from trade union leader to political party leader. Eventually they smoothed things over; nevertheless, some of the tensions remain.

There are some ANC members who like to declare that "the Alliance will never break up, not for fifty years". Which seems a logically deficient and/or agenda-led prediction, given that Cosatu didn't even exist thirty years ago. Anyone who predicts politics that far ahead – including those who make predictions "until Jesus comes" – is simply wrong. If the Alliance does fracture in the short- to medium-term future, it seems likely that the rift will come between the ANC and Cosatu, as the SACP appears to have aligned itself so closely to the ANC in recent years. Then again, perhaps that very fact, and the resulting loss in its political voice and credibility, will lead to a dramatic change of direction when the SACP's current leadership moves on.

Why this really matters
It's still possible that if there is a strong oppositionist movement to the ANC, it could come from the Alliance – if, or when, it breaks up.

Why this really matters *now*
The debates that normally happen in public in other countries, between different political organisations, actually happen behind closed doors in South Africa, within the Alliance. In Britain there might be a tussle over economic policy between Labour and the Conservatives; in South Africa, it's between parts of the ANC and the SACP and Cosatu, all behind the scenes. But the fights and the debates do happen, which is why we all spend so much time reading Sunday newspaper stories about fights within the Alliance – because they're the real pointers to what kind of policy or direction the ANC and the government will take in the future.

As such, the Alliance provides a level of opposition to ANC leaders' political space. While it sometimes looks like the ANC, Cosatu and the SACP agree on everything, they don't. And their arrangement ensures that the ANC doesn't have all the power in government. For example, if there was no Alliance, it's likely the Protection of State Information Bill would already be law, and we'd be paying to use the highways between Johannesburg and Pretoria. Cosatu strongly opposes both, and its place in the Alliance means that they haven't yet happened.

Democratic Alliance / DA

Founded: 1959 (or 2000; take your pick)
Motto: Building an open opportunity society for all

The ANC's official opposition; leaders of the "equal opportunity society"; to some, "the whites who want to bring back apartheid"; to others, "the future of the country"

The DA is the party that will tell you it will rule South Africa one day. It may be right, it may be wrong (it may be crazy); it's too early to say. But it is certainly right to tell you that it is the only party that has been growing in voting numbers during all recent elections. (That said, it is not growing in actual party membership numbers, while the ANC's membership has rocketed recently.)

Timeline

1960s	1970s	1989	2000	2009
Suzman only MP in Parliament.	Becomes PRP then PFP.	Becomes DP under De Beer.	DA merges with NNP, under Leon.	Wins W. Cape under Zille.

History

Parties change over time as history and circumstances dictate – and sometimes it takes a while for one to find its feet. The ANC was once the South African Native National Congress; the SACP was once the Communist Party of South Africa. The DA, on the other hand, was once the Progressive Party (PP), then it was the Progressive Reform Party (PRP), then it was the Progressive Federal Party (PFP), then it was the Democratic Party (DP), then it was the Democratic Alliance… Even as the DA, it has evolved, rebranded and reinvented itself.

What we now know as the DA was formed in 1959 as a breakaway of the then United Party. After the 1961 elections, Helen Suzman was the only representative of the new party who remained an MP, and she was famously Parliament's lone (white, Jewish, female) voice against apartheid policies for over a decade.

After 1990, the then-PFP party rebranded itself as the Democratic Party and, though winning a relatively small share of the vote in 1994, started to professionalise itself, making as much noise as possible, as well as the occasional constitutional point here and there.

This was a crucial time for the country and the future of our politics. By then Tony Leon was DP leader and the ANC was officially in a government of national unity with the National Party and Inkatha Freedom Party. Leon chose not to join the government, despite being

The first Helen
Helen Zille may be the face of the new DA, but Helen Suzman is the party's Mandela. Her moral rectitude famously irked the Nats back in the day and she was twice nominated for the Nobel Peace Prize (though she was not faultless). She died in 2009, but is still making the news. In 2013 the "Know Your DA" campaign, featuring a poster of Mandela embracing Suzman, was criticised by the ANC as propaganda that "elevated" her to a struggle hero. It all turned out to be a good example of the lengths both parties will go to to retrospectively position themselves.

GROOTES POWER RATING ™

asked to do so by Nelson Mandela, who offered him a Cabinet position in the process. Leon's condition was that he would join only if he could still speak out against Cabinet decisions he disagreed with, while Mandela felt it was important that ministers speak with one voice. Leon felt his main role should be to create a proper opposition in South Africa, and so he declined the offer – which meant the DP was the only party in Parliament and outside the government's tent at the same time.

Think about that for a moment. Mandela himself offers you a Cabinet spot, and you say no. That's quite a decision. But Leon has probably been vindicated: South Africa now has a growing opposition, which may not have happened if he had said yes. Certainly if the subsequent fortunes of the NP and IFP are anything to go by, it was a prescient call.

After the 1999 elections, which saw the New National Party lose support, Leon entered into an alliance with the party, then led by Marthinus van Schalkwyk. This is where the A in DA comes from. But Van Schalkwyk, having already turned traitor once on his party ideals, then took the NNP out of the DA to form an alliance with the ANC. The ANC wanted to rule the Western Cape and he had the key to making that happen.

It was a self-serving and rather desperate move on Van Schalkwyk's behalf, and proved as much when the majority of his supporters stayed with the DA. And he's been punished ever since by being given all the power that comes with being Tourism minister, and being able to watch ANC NEC meetings happen without being able to speak during them.

Leon, though, powered ahead, sailing through various controversies and emerging as the main public voice against the ANC and Mandela's successor, Thabo Mbeki. The criticisms he faced during his time in charge included heated reactions to the DA's "Fight Back" campaign in 1999 (read as "fight black" in some quarters) and the "whites only" and even "men only" allegations of his running of the party. Mbeki, for one, really didn't like him – to the point where it emerged, as Leon was stepping down as DA leader in 2007, that he and Mbeki had never met in a one-on-one meeting. Mbeki quickly arranged tea and cakes, sensing he probably looked a little small on this.

In August 2007, as the winds were blowing towards Polokwane, Leon resigned and Helen Zille was elected DA leader. She had been building momentum for some time, and had easily the most professional lobbying team in the party. Since then the DA has grown strongly. In the final weeks of the 2009 election campaign, it used "Stop Zuma" as a slogan, which was criticised in some circles as being "uncomfortably reminiscent" of Leon's "Fight Back" slogan – but, you know, there were some people who bought into it this time around.

The DA gained 16.6 percent of the vote that time around, and took 24 percent in the 2011 local government elections. Put those numbers in perspective: the 2009 result reflects one in six South Africans voting for the DA, jumping to one in four in 2011. These may well be damned statistics, with all that they entail, but given that only one in eleven South Africans is white, it's hard to argue against the DA's contention that it is no longer a "whites only" party.

There are several recent trends that really matter to the DA.

First, white people started to register to vote, and then took the trouble to vote. By 2011, as Julius Malema was doing his utmost to damage the ANC, many other minority groups also started to register. In short, people who had been seen as "brown, but politically black" became "brown, but politically white". In municipal elections you can examine

Insulting the DA (previously very easy, getting harder)

"The DA will bring back apartheid." – general ANC criticism

"Voting for the DA is voting for the Madam." – Julius Malema, c.2011

"A vote for the National Development Plan is a vote for the DA." – NUMSA, c.2013 which way wards voted, and thus you can clearly work out how coloured and Indian areas started to vote for the DA for the first time.

Of course the DA thinks it can continue this trend, but its next task is going to be harder.

The future

The DA's next major hurdle is convincing the urban black middle class to vote for it. The ANC is well aware of this; it's no coincidence Cyril Ramaphosa was elected ANC deputy leader at Mangaung.

The real question in our politics, which affects the DA more than anyone, is how long "identity politics" will last. Once upon a bad old time, race and class lines were effectively the same things; the rise of the Black Diamond indicates that this is no longer the case. So how long will it be before people stop voting along racial lines, and along class lines? We're seeing it happen, and when it starts it's a process that may gain momentum more quickly than expected, simply because around the world history tells us that class interests really matter the most when making political decisions.

Which is not to say, by any means, that the DA will automatically become the next party of government. There are many possibilities, and at some point along the road the DA may well change its identity entirely. Zille has made a lot of progress forming coalitions in local government, and will be keen to repeat the experience in a few provinces. Meanwhile more parties are emerging, and some of them – probably not the EFF – could be useful if they joined the DA and thus started to help change its public identity.

Stephen Grootes 2014 DA national election prediction

24%

That the DA is growing is undeniable, but it still has many twists to go in its possible path to power. Can it actually win the 2019 elections? Is this remotely possible? You'd think not, but we'll have a better idea after Elections 2014.

Helen Zille

Born: 9 March 1951

*Leader of the DA; premier of the Western Cape; anti-apartheid
activist; journalist; Godzille of Western Cape politics*

Helen Zille is often so strident in her criticism of the ANC that it's easy
to forget she was also one of those who quite literally put themselves
and their futures on the line in the fight against apartheid. As with most
politicians who were journalists in their early life, she has an innate and
clear sense of what societies are looking for. She also has the ability to

Timeline

1977	1996	2007	2008	2009
Uncovers Biko murder conspiracy.	Joins DA.	Assumes DA leadership.	Voted World Mayor of the Year.	Becomes premier of Western Cape.

POWER | MORAL

GROOTES POWER RATING ™

think quickly, and she is fierce in her defence of what she believes in.

Past

Otta Helene Zille grew up in Hillbrow in central Johannesburg, and attended the prestigious St Mary's School. She was politically conscious from a young age, and entered political life through her employment as a reporter at the *Rand Daily Mail* in the 1970s. It was there that she first came to national prominence when she played a key role in perhaps the greatest journalistic scoop in South African history, the revelation that Steve Biko had been murdered in police custody *(see sidebar opposite)*. Zille later resigned from newspapers, but she continued her anti-apartheid activities through the Black Sash and various other organisations.

It was actually through her two young boys that she then re-entered the political world years later. She was on the governing body of their government school in Cape Town in 1996 when she refused to accept a government ruling limiting the powers of school bodies over teacher appointments. Zille being Zille, it turned into quite a fight. She won, the DP noticed her, and she agreed to join them.

By 2006 she'd become mayor of Cape Town, having to negotiate a series of tenuous coalitions. Initially dependent on other smaller parties, she was eventually able to ensure a full DA majority in the city. (In this, she was ably assisted by the ANC in the Western Cape, who had decided that a good old-fashioned implosion was due; it still hasn't recovered.)

The following year, when Tony Leon moved on and the DA went through a small Polokwane of its own, she became the party's leader. At Gallagher Estate in Midrand, it was clear early on that most of the delegates were behind her. It was also apparent that claims that the DA was a "white party" were simply wrong, and that the majority of "non-white" DA members were clearly behind Zille, despite having two other candidates they could back. Her internal campaign was also far more professional than any other leadership campaign the party had ever seen.

And once she was in charge, it was clear the DA was moving up a notch. The party had more energy and a different attitude. Leon had done an excellent job of establishing an opposition and of ensuring it would remain a permanent feature on our political scene; Zille saw her job as positioning the party to actually govern in certain areas.

Her first aim was to take the Western Cape itself. This the party achieved relatively easily in 2009. At national level, she was also able to use the anti-Zuma feeling against the ANC quite effectively, leading to the surge in DA support around the country.

Meanwhile, within the DA itself, her power base was strengthening. In politics, as in most things, nothing succeeds like success. If you win more political power in government, you almost always win more political power within your party. And this happened to Zille. People she wanted in key positions suddenly started to win internal elections.

Present

In person Zille is the consummate politician. She will never let her guard down with you. She is aware that everything she says and does is on the record. And she's very, very clear

The Biko scoop

When news of Steve Biko's death emerged in September 1977, the public were told it was the result of a hunger strike, Justice Minister Jimmy Kruger famously declaring that "*dit laat my koud*". But the 26-year-old Zille was one of those convinced the government was lying. Once she had her facts straight, the nation was delivered the news beneath the *Rand Daily Mail* headline "No Sign of Hunger Strike – Biko Doctors". Such was the power of the Nats that they were able to force the Press Council to convict her of "tendentious reporting". The paper was even forced to publish a "correction".

How to address her: "Madam Premier", on the first meeting. "Helen" thereafter.

Answer to a tough question: Blame the ANC, or compare it to her party.

Morning wake-up time: Long before you.

about where she stands on everything. Which means she is prepared for almost every possible question. Many a journalist has tried to trip her up, only to watch in great personal anguish as she uses a carefully crafted question to rip apart the ANC. Many journalists are intimidated by her, and you certainly don't want to be the one in the room asking a question based on an incorrect fact. She's also not scared to ring you up if you print something she disagrees with.

Zille also thinks ahead more than most. The decision to donate a million rand to the Opposition to Urban Tolling Alliance (Outa) is a good example. While at first it looked like an opportunistic bid by a political party to get involved in the e-tolling debate, what it actually did was make tolling an election issue for 2014. The ANC can't oppose the decision because it's the party that wants to toll Gauteng's highways.

Under Zille the DA has grown quite quickly, taking power in the Western Cape and ramping up its activities in Gauteng. This has been based on her drive to make issues of "service delivery, service delivery, service delivery" dominate our politics. Of course she hasn't quite succeeded in that, but she's made a huge impact.

Likely future

Zille is one of those rare politicians willing to put her heart and soul into the game even when she knows she has no chance whatsoever of becoming president. She also knows that at some point, probably pretty soon, the DA will need to have someone in charge who is less blonde to take it to the next level. That said, barring any major political calamities, her performance in getting the DA into power at the local and provincial level means she will always be historically important to her party.

Lindiwe Mazibuko

Born: 9 April 1980
DA Parliamentary leader; voice of the
opposition to Nkandla and government
corruption; a "coconut"

Technically, Lindiwe Mazibuko's job is simply to lead the DA in Parliament; in other words, she is the official voice of the opposition in the National Assembly. But her role goes far deeper than that. This being South Africa, the fact she, as a black woman, beat Athol Trollip, a white man, for the job was a pivotal moment in the DA's evolution from "white party" to "equal opportunity society".

But for Mazibuko it was actually only a small step up. In a moment of political genius, Mazibuko had been appointed national spokeswoman for the DA in 2009. In other words, her face and voice were seen and heard constantly around the country. It was an early indicator that the DA was changing, and was no longer a majority "white" party.

Mazibuko came to politics through the less-than-traditional route of writing an academic paper on then-new Cape Town mayor Helen Zille. After graduating, she was employed by the party as a spokesperson and researcher. From there, as her profile grew and her brain began to be noticed, it was a matter of time before she was promoted.

She has repeatedly been accused by parts of the ANC of being a coconut (black on the outside, white on the inside), but she has shown she is more than tough enough to survive these attacks. Even when facing the most extreme provocation from the most extreme of characters, like Julius Malema – who called her a tea-girl on national television to her face – she has been able to keep her calm. Key to her responses is the supreme ability to count to ten before speaking, whereafter she can not only put a Malema back in his place, but actually use the opportunity to explain that in the DA no-one speaks like that, and that identity doesn't matter in her party. It's very clever, and requires huge amounts of EQ to pull off.

GROOTES POWER RATING ™

There were some concerns Mazibuko would simply be too young to pull off her new role. She was 31 when she took it up and, after all, a knowledge of parliamentary tactics and skullduggery is usually the most useful thing in the position. But she's shown herself to be more than able. The DA will often lose the vote but win the media war afterwards due to her skills.

Likely future

Mazibuko has been hailed as a "rising star" so often she must be quite sick of the tag. While many people have suggested she could well lead the DA at some point, Mmusi Maimane (*below*) seems the more likely contender for now. For the moment though, Mazibuko is one of the key national figures within the DA, and will likely be around for many years to come.

Mmusi Maimane
Born: 6 June 1980
DA spokesperson; leader of the party in Johannesburg; its next leader, fullstop?

At the beginning of 2011 you'd have to have been a really close follower of our politics to know who Mmusi Maimane was. By the end of the year, you would have had to have been a hermit – especially if you lived in Gauteng – not to recognise him immediately.

What changed is that the DA, in one of those characteristically clever moves, had spotted talent, groomed it well, and only then put it on stage. Maimane was picked to be the party's mayoral candidate for Joburg, and while it was never likely he would win, it would give him a huge platform.

So, clutching his iPhone tightly, he jumped in with both feet.

Then, after the ANC won in the city, Helen Zille appointed him national spokesperson of the DA – which immediately made him one of the busiest people in the country, and one of the more prominent.

Being the spokesperson for an opposition party that lives by the amount of media attention it can generate requires someone who is sharp and can turn a debate on its head in a split second, and yet avoid further controversy. It's not easy. Maimane does it with aplomb, while managing to campaign to grow his party all at the same time.

If there is one blot on his copybook, it's that the very real problems in the City of Johannesburg could do with some more of his attention. Anyone who lives there will tell you all about its finance problems; the city sometimes seems to just make up its bills. Given that it's the sight of a very real political contest, Maimane could be accused of not spending enough time in the caucus and making sure that these are a top priority.

Likely future

In August 2013 Maimane was announced as the DA's Gauteng premier candidate for the 2014 election. There are many who believe he is going to eventually run the party itself. He's young, he has time on his side, and he seems to straddle the cultural divides between white and black very easily. Being married to a white woman helps. For the DA, this is the key issue. He's able to resonate with the Hurlingham madam while also talking directly to the heart of Soweto, where he grew up. You may even hear that his parents still live there. It's true, and it gives him a legitimacy that the ANC cannot take away.

But Maimane could still make mistakes considering that in politics – as in sport – youth and skill are no match for age and treachery. If he is careful with what he does, the sky is literally the limit for him. Helen Zille will never be president of South Africa; but there are worse bets than Mmusi Maimane.

GROOTES POWER RATING ™

Inkatha Freedom Party / IFP

Founded: 1975

One-time Zulu-nationalist voter enclave;
once-influential political party; Buthelezi's pet project

In the early 1990s it seemed the IFP, and its leader, Mangosuthu Buthelezi, had the power to tear the country apart. In the run-up to the first democratic elections, tensions between the IFP and the ANC, with even deeper rifts between Zulu- and Xhosa-speaking people, exploded into violence in KwaZulu-Natal and Gauteng. Back then the IFP had enough support to win KZN with its strong Zulu-nationalist appeal; Buthelezi was made deputy president of the country and acted as president numerous times. Since then, the party's decline has been dramatic, and it's because the IFP has imploded that the ANC has managed to grow its support in KZN so quickly – which is why the ANC has retained its share of the national vote while its support in other provinces has dropped.

**Stephen Grootes
2014 IFP national
election prediction**

3%

Buthelezi himself, a man famous for extraordinarily long-winded speeches and for playing Cetshwayo in the film *Zulu* in 1964, is mainly to blame for this. It's been a one-man party for nearly forty years now; he's refused to give up power, anoint a successor, or move with the times. And he's been punished for that, with the IFP slipping to just 4.5 percent in the national polls. The party has also split, after its former national chairperson, Zanele kaMagwaza-Msibi, left to form the National Freedom Party. Tensions between the IFP and the NFP have now spilt over into violence.

Likely future

As long as Buthelezi, now in his mid 80s, refuses to change, the IFP is likely to simply head into oblivion. It's only if he goes, and the party is able to somehow renew itself, that it could start to contend for power in KZN again. And then only if a post-Zuma ANC somehow starts to slip up in the province.

The African Christian Democratic Party / ACDP

Founded: 1993

Religious conservatives; the party of the righteous; Meshoe's pet project

Every country has a political party that wants to ban things it doesn't like. The ACDP wants to get rid of abortion, homosexual acts and gay marriage.

It also wants to rename Devil's Peak. So far, thankfully, they have not been very successful.

Under Reverend Kenneth Meshoe, the party has played a role in various parliamentary committees over the years, querying legislation that it disagreed with. For that alone it still has some relevance, and is shown a modicum of respect by the other opposition parties.

Likely future

Like other smaller parties, the ACDP's share of the vote has declined dramatically in recent times. It won only three seats in 2009, which equates to 0.8 percent of the vote. It may do even worse in 2014.

Freedom Front Plus / FF+

Founded: 1994

Afrikaner voter enclave; fighter for Afrikaner rights; the most right-wing party in the country; Mulder's pet project

Look, it's not exactly the AWB, but the Freedom Front Plus – more likely to be referred to as *die Vryheidsfront Plus* by its supporters – is what you might call the last hold-out for those who voted National Party for all those years and simply cannot bring themselves to vote for anyone else. Polling data suggests that's about 150,000 voters; not a great percentage considering 23 million people are registered to vote. If you're a betting man you'd give low odds that about 99 percent of them, give or take, are white. And probably Afrikaans-speaking.

Stephen Grootes 2014 FF+ national election prediction

<1%

As always with a small party, it lives or dies by the public image of its leader. Originally, that was General Constand Viljoen, who cobbled together a workable coalition of the small parties fighting for the same Afrikaner vote just before the 1994 elections. Nowadays, the FF+ is blessed to have Dr Pieter Mulder in charge. A former Communications professor at Potchefstroom University, he's articulate, clever and politically astute. Unfortunately his knowledge of history appears to be lacking at times. He seems to believe there were no black people in most of South Africa before the white settlers came. (Amazing what apartheid education can do to history.)

He himself has also struck it lucky in that the ANC offered him a position as deputy minister in the Department of Agriculture, Forestry and Fisheries. This makes the ANC appear big and reconciliatory, and gives him a nice public platform, which he's not afraid to use.

Likely future

The FF+ will survive as long as its leader is able to stay relevant and meaningful. Should it lose Mulder, it's not inconceivable that it could just disappear altogether. Its existence is useful for the DA, as it makes the official opposition look less right wing and more moderate, and Helen Zille can spit her fury at the "racism displayed by the FF+" when the need arises.

United Democratic Movement / UDM

Founded: 1997

Once-exciting alternative voting option; now alternative Xhosa voting option; Holomisa's pet project

The UDM had a great start. Back in 1997 it seemed this was the party that would really deracialise South Africa (a country where the word "deracialise" exists). Bantu Holomisa and Roelf Meyer, both politically strong men, with histories in the ANC and NP respectively, helmed it. But the ANC was simply too dominant, and able to keep the UDM's share of the vote down to around 3.5 percent. In time, Meyer resigned, taking most of his former NP friends with him.

Holomisa has ploughed on, with his core vote coming from the area around the old Transkei in the Eastern Cape, where he was "president" for several years in the bad old days.

**Stephen Grootes
2014 UDM national
election prediction**

1%

Likely future

The UDM is unlikely to have much impact on the national stage. Holomisa has made it known he'd like to form a coalition with other parties, but it seems his ego hasn't yet found the political partner willing to give him all the power but not the responsibility.

Congress of the People / Cope

Founded: 2008

Once-headline-grabbing alternative voting option; Mbeki's rejects;
Lekota's pet project

Founded after the first real post-apartheid split within the ANC, Cope
was expected to be the party that finally gave the urban, educated black
voter a genuine voting alternative. There was chaos within the ANC
during and after its 2007 Polokwane conference, and the madness boiled
over with the 2008 recall of President Thabo Mbeki. Cope emerged
from the ashes shortly afterwards, essentially a group of Mbeki-ites who
couldn't stand Jacob Zuma and knew they'd be left out in the cold under
his regime. They were the Polokwane losers, led by former ANC chair
Mosiuoa Lekota and former premier of Gauteng Mbhazima Shilowa.

After their first full conference in December 2008, Cope hit the
campaign trail hard and was able to win around 7.5 percent of the
vote – not as much as many blindly optimistic/naïve followers thought
it might, but a sizeable chunk nonetheless. A small party like Cope,
however, simply wasn't ever going to be big enough to constrain the egos
of Shilowa and Lekota, and so the squabbling began. There was public
slanging, legal wrangling and, eventually, Polokwane-esque chaos. By
the 2011 local government elections, the party was unable to organise
itself and had lost virtually all its moral credibility; as a result, its share
of the vote collapsed.

Stephen Grootes
2014 Cope national election prediction

3%

Likely future

Lekota now seems intent to soldier on on his own. But it seems unlikely he will be able to really make much headway on his own, given what's gone before.

Cope's share of the vote is likely to drop dramatically at the 2014 national elections, with its remaining supporters giving Agang a bash or simply scuttling back to the safety of the ANC.

National Freedom Party / NFP

Founded: 2011

IFP off-shoot/heir; KaMagwaza-Msibi's pet project

The NFP is to the IFP what Cope is to the ANC. In other words, a split caused by a leadership tussle. Zanele KaMagwaza-Msibi was the chair of the IFP who became annoyed when she realised Buthelezi was never going to relinquish power. Initially written off at its launch in 2011, the party has managed to make relatively impressive progress, but predictably only in

KZN. The two parties' supporters tend to clash violently from time to time, and the leaders of neither choose to condemn that violence.

Likely future

KaMagwaza-Msibi's first outing during the 2011 local government elections saw her earn 10 percent of the vote in KZN, a not insignificant figure in a populous province. But she will regard it only as a foundation, and will be looking to surpass the IFP in the future.

Stephen Grootes 2014 NFP national election prediction

2%

Economic Freedom Fighters / EFF

Founded: 2013

What Julius did next; red-beret-wearing revolutionaries; Malema's pet project

Some people think the Economic Freedom Fighters are going to be the next big thing; that the party is going to tap into the anger and frustration of a large group of people whose lives haven't changed since 1994. That

**Stephen Grootes
2014 EFF
national election
prediction**

1 %

there is anger and frustration is clearly right. That Julius Malema can make something of it is (even more) clearly wrong.

While Malema still gets media headlines and hasn't lost his gift of the gab, the fact is he's going to really struggle to get it going. There are plenty of people who could and would support the EFF under the right circumstances. Problem is, a party of any stripe needs organisation and structure. And this is what the EFF lacks. The only person in its leadership anyone's ever heard of is Malema. That's because there is no-one else. (For a brief collaborative moment, controversial sushi-eater and ex-convict Kenny Kunene was the other famous name in the party, but even he abandoned ship when reality set in.) This means that when it comes to actually getting things done – you know, organising events, canvassing voters, coming up with policy – there is no-one to do it.

Beyond this logistical difficulty, Malema's history in the ANC Youth League shows that he is a bully who doesn't tolerate other opinions. As a result, it is going to be impossible for him to build up the brains trust anyone in politics actually needs.

This is a pity, because it's important to keep those frustrated with the current parties involved in parliamentary politics. A party like EFF could work under the right circumstances. These are not them.

Likely future

In reality, it seems the only reason the EFF exists is to provide Malema with an excuse to claim the corruption charges he faces in Limpopo are a "political conspiracy". Those charges are serious. And even if there has been political motivation in making sure they are pursued, if any of them stick – and they seem very likely to – Malema will be heading to jail. When he does, there is unlikely to be a huge crowd waving him off.

Agang

Founded: 2013

*Anti-corruption campaigners; a vision of something or other;
Ramphele's pet project*

Yet another voice of the voiceless, Agang was started by Dr Mamphela
Ramphele in 2013, mainly out of her anger and frustration with the
ANC. Part of this appears to be personal enmity against Jacob Zuma,
and much of it seems to be principled. Ramphele feels there is a large
enough group of people who are frustrated with the corruption and
nepotism in the current ANC to vote against it and, having spoken out
against the government regularly over the years, has finally put her (not
inconsiderable) money where her mouth is.

Ramphele is famously associated with Steve Biko, and Agang is also an
attempt for her to get back to her Black Consciousness Movement roots,
which preach self-reliance. However the party started life powered by
ideals, rather than structure or political experience. The former is fine, but
there needs to be a load of the latter if it is to succeed.

Likely future

There is certainly a large group of people who are frustrated with the
corruption and nepotism in the current ANC, but their all voting for
Agang seems rather unlikely. There is something of a rule in South African

Stephen Grootes 2014 Agang national election prediction

3%

politics that suggests that in 1999 a certain group of people voted for the UDM, in 2004 that group voted for the Independent Democrats, and in 2009 they voted for Cope. In 2014 they may well vote for Agang. But no-one really knows.

Due to its lack of structure, it's going to be very difficult for Agang to fight the 2014 elections properly. Perhaps the good doctor Ramphele has some aces up her sleeve…

SIU **HIV/ Aids**

Toilet wars

Nkandla Blue-light brigades

Shaik **Zuma** R70 billion

Police incompetence Spy tapes

The Arms Deal R206 million

Marikana Mugabe National Key Points Act

The Guptas Poo flinging Secrecy Bill

Richard Mdluli

Zimbabwe NPA

Waterkloof

Controversies!

As South Africans we like to think we're different, that somehow we, and our politics, are unique. That's purely natural. After all, we lived through a unique set of circumstances. Look at the countries that went through the Tunisian-style revolutions now and see how difficult they're finding their massive changes in government. For us, it was easy. A bit of Madiba magic, Cyril and Roelf go fishing and – hey presto! – the Constitution arrives. Not really, but you get the picture.

The wars of our country have, however, continued, just by other means. So the fight against the fact that only whites were rich in 1994 continues, and the fight against land redistribution is still with us.

Which gives our controversies a certain flavour. There's a certain level of outrage that we all have, anger perhaps, at the past. Add to that a massive and growing split in the views and opinions of people who live in urban and rural areas, plus a party in power that comes close to total dominance, and hysteria can be expected.

Some controversies are simply natural and obvious errors of government, like the Arms Deal. Some are very South African; say, the Zuma spy tapes. And some are completely universal, and could be found in any country, like Nkandla.

But it's important to remember, every country has outrage, every country has scandal, and all politics can be termed controversial in some or other way. We South Africans just take it to a whole new level. Because we are unique...

These are the important controversies that have shaped and reflect our current political landscape.

Government's HIV/Aids policy
Or: South Africa's modern genocide; when Thabo spent too long on the internet
First erupted: 1999

Having sparked perhaps the most frenzied controversy bar none since 1994, it's amazing how uncontroversial the topic of HIV and Aids is these days. Once upon a time any public discussion on the matter was underscored with all sorts of angst and outrage and powerlessness at our government's official position on it. Now, while the disease itself remains a blight, our policy on how to deal with it is a complete non-issue. Which is perhaps the strongest proof that Thabo Mbeki was simply wrong about it all along.

The controversy has its origins back in the early days of the Mbeki presidency, when he started to publicly question the link between HIV and Aids. It appeared that many of the facts he was using came from internet sites and people who were not recognised as experts by medical authorities. (Matthias Rath, for example, is a German vitamin pedlar with international court rulings against him for false advertising and defamation.) But it was Minister of Health Manto Tshabalala-Msimang who Mbeki let take the flak for most of what he thought. She was the one who became known as Dr Beetroot, claiming that olive oil, lemon and various vegetables were better for Aids sufferers than antiretroviral drugs, and opposing the introduction of Nevirapine, which was proven to stop the transmission of HIV from mothers to their unborn children. Eventually, the Treatment Action Campaign, headed by Zackie Achmat, was able to convince the Constitutional Court to force Mbeki's government to provide the life-saving drug to mothers in government hospitals.

Having stumbled when discussing the issue early in his presidency – he famously told *Time* in 2000 that "the notion that immune deficiency is only acquired from a single virus cannot be sustained"– Mbeki later stayed aloof and out of the fray, leaving Tshabalala-Msimang to do her worst. That same year she refused to answer questions about her beliefs, instead telling off John Robbie on Talk Radio 702 with the line "I'm not Manto to you!" and insisting that what she believed was medically correct. She would stubbornly push Mbeki's line for a further eight years, despite international condemnation and ever-mounting evidence that South Africa's world-leading infection rates were a national (and humanitarian) disaster.

In 2007 Tshabalala-Msimang was hospitalised and, almost incredibly, received a liver transplant in a government hospital, despite well-publicised allegations that she had a drinking problem. While there was widespread cynicism about the fact she was able to get the transplant ahead of other more viable candidates, no-one was ever able to produce a smoking gun proving she had jumped the queue. It was a bizarre tangent in the long-running story. Two years later, Tshabalala-Msimang was dead and government policy on Aids treatment had changed drastically.

From an internal ANC point of view, it was clear Zuma was going to change things when he told an audience just ten days before Polokwane, "We need to declare a state of emergency on Aids and crime." It was obvious that the majority of the ANC was unhappy with Mbeki's stance, and after he was recalled from the Presidency in 2008 Barbara Hogan replaced Tshabalala-Msimang at the Department of Health on a caretaker basis. There was singing in the streets. Hogan immediately started the process of implementing a new HIV/Aids policy, and later that year a Harvard study concluded that the Mbeki-era Aids policy had caused 330,000 avoidable deaths.

It is to Zuma's great credit that almost the first thing he did as president was appoint the brilliant Aaron Motsoaledi to take over from Hogan, and then arrange well-publicised displays of public Aids testing. Zuma himself was tested, along with many of his ministers. As a result, public attitudes to HIV and Aids have started to change. More importantly, public hospitals hand out ARVs to almost all who need them, all HIV infection rate indicators have improved since 2008, and life expectancy in South Africa has jumped enormously, apparently because of this change in policy alone.

> "Does HIV cause Aids? Can a virus cause a syndrome? How? It can't, because a syndrome is a group of diseases resulting from acquired immune deficiency."
>
> – Thabo Mbeki, answering a question in Parliament, September 2000

Mbeki and his fellow travellers on the Aids issue have faded off in to the sunset, and hopefully will never be heard from again on this issue. Though the controversy is over, the legacy of their failed policy will remain for generations, most obviously in the shape of our current orphan epidemic and preponderance of child-headed households.

The Arms Deal
Or: The ANC's original sin in power;
South Africa's golden calf
First erupted: 1999

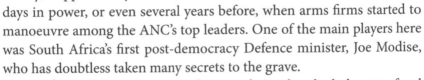

The Arms Deal is the ANC's original sin in power. The events and processes that have spun out of it have managed to infect almost the very fibre of the party's being, and we are still living with its effects today, most notably in the fact that our current president was (is) accused, but has not stood trial for, corruption.

While the roots of the Defence ministry's Strategic Defence Procurement of 1999 are murky, it appears they lie almost in the ANC's first days in power, or even several years before, when arms firms started to manoeuvre among the ANC's top leaders. One of the main players here was South Africa's first post-democracy Defence minister, Joe Modise, who has doubtless taken many secrets to the grave.

From early on, the amount of money being bandied about to fund new frigates, submarines and fighter jets was so large that many questions were raised. The cost at the time was pegged at more than R30 billion, to be paid off by 2018; it has subsequently risen to more than R70 billion, according to some estimates. In Parliament even members of the ANC, such as Andrew Feinstein, opposed the deal once details started emerging. But the orders came from on high, through Thabo Mbeki, Jacob Zuma and others, that the deal must continue despite suggestions of improprieties. Feinstein, who subsequently wrote perhaps the preeminent book on the arms deal, *After The Party*, estimates that more than $300 million was paid in bribes to facilitate it. (He has now left the country and lives in London, where he has become an expert on the international arms trade.)

ARMS DEAL DETAILS

The three major acquisitions of the 1999 arms deal were for ships, submarines and a jet trainers/jet fighters package

	WHAT WE WERE LOOKING TO BUY	ORIGINAL PREFERRED BIDDERS	WHAT WE GOT (1999 PRICING)	CURRENT STATUS	ESTIMATED COST AS OF 2013
SHIPS	5 x corvettes	Spain's Bazan light frigate cheapest, complied with most criteria	4 x Meko A-200 SAN frigates, via German Frigate Consortium cost: R6.9 billion	Operational ability restricted due to budget constraints and personnel shortages; only 2 ships operational at a time; reports of engine troubles, reliability and maintenance problems	R13.5 billion
SUBMARINES	4 x patrol submarines	Italy's Fincantieri apparently preferred by the Navy	3 x Type 209 submarines, via German Submarine Consortium cost: R5.4 billion	1 vessel "out of service" since 2007; personnel constraints result in only 1 vessel operational at a time, at times none; fleet spends two-thirds of its time in dock	R11 billion
JETS	24 x LIFT (lead-in fighter trainers); 48 x ALFA (advanced light fighter aircraft)	Italy's Aermacchi clear LIFT winner; of 3 ALFA contenders, Gripen "not affordable"	24 x BAE Hawks trainers from UK; 26 x Saab Gripen fighters from Sweden cost: R19.6 billion	Only an estimated 6–9 qualified Gripen pilots in SAAF; at least 12 Gripens currently in long-term storage; estimated half of remaining planes operational	R40 billion

There have been several glaring avenues of suspicion, but the most damning is that in some of the deals neither the lowest nor the most well-reviewed bidders won the contract. In the case of the purchase of BAE Hawk jet trainers and SAAB Gripen fighters, easily the most expensive contract within the overall deal, the equipment in question didn't even make the original shortlists and was specifically not wanted by the Air

Force. Today only a handful of the Gripens are operational, with about half in long-term storage.

Which is to say, we paid (way) too much for the wrong equipment.

The bribery allegations have been varied and numerous, but the most high-profile claims were those relating to Zuma and his advisors. Eventually charges were laid against Schabir Shaik but not Zuma, despite then National Prosecuting Authority head Bulelani Ngcuka proclaiming he had "prima facie evidence of corruption" against him. Shaik, Zuma's financial advisor at the time, was accused of arranging a bribe for his employer from a French arms company. He was found guilty of being in cahoots with Zuma in 2005, with the quite explicit corollary conclusion being that Zuma had been in cahoots with Shaik. A week later Mbeki removed Zuma from his position as deputy president. He also tried to force him to resign as deputy president of the ANC. But at the ANC's National General Council, which was underway at the time, ANC members refused to accept Zuma's resignation, so he stayed in office.

This was the genesis of the Zuma and Mbeki animosity; before, they had been long-time comrades and friends, having been on the run together in the bad old days. While Zuma was eventually charged, the charges against him were then withdrawn on the legally dubious grounds that Ngcuka may have interfered with the timing of the charges after he had left his office at the NPA. The basis for this ruling was the infamous Zuma spy tapes, which purport to show interference in the case *(see p218)*.

The consensus of those in the know is that both Mbeki and Zuma have been privy to the dodgy behind-the-scenes arms-deal goings on. Mbeki may not have taken money directly, but he appears to have condoned it by covering for Modise and possibly the ANC in general. Many others within the ANC have been accused of corruption relating to the deal at one time or another. But the Shaik conviction and a brief prison spell served by Tony Yengeni notwithstanding, none of this has been proven – so government today goes about its business as though all those fingered, many of them in the corridors of power, are upstanding and virtuous citizens.

In 2011 Zuma appointed the Seriti Commission of Inquiry to investigate the entire issue, with a mandate to get to the bottom of it. Almost immediately is also ran into controversy. A senior investigator at the commission, Norman Moabi, quit, with his resignation letter claiming the commission was following a "second agenda". This phrase has haunted the commission ever since as other officials have resigned and Judge Francis Legodi has stepped down for "personal reasons" that have not been disclosed.

Meanwhile time marches on and it seems that another high-profile politician being brought to book on the matter is as likely as the SAAF actually putting all 26 of its Gripens into service at the same time – unless something comes of the Zuma spy tapes. In all likelihood we will never know what really happened, and who took money from whom and for whom.

The Zimbabwe crisis
Or: The dictator next door;
Mad Bob up north
First erupted: 2000

Zimbabwean politics has always had a special place in our politics because it's a country that became free before us, and because the economic disaster that's unfolded there in the last decade and more has led to an enormous number of Zimbabweans living among us – possibly as many as five million – and thus had a very real impact on our economy. Another prime reason is because the land grabs that have occurred across our northern border stare certain groups in our country right in the face. That is, they scare the hell out of South Africa's white population and encourage people like Julius Malema to scare them even more by trying to do the same thing.

As a result, since the start of Thabo Mbeki's "quiet diplomacy" in the 2000s, to Zuma's attempts to mediate there more recently, our government has been strongly criticised for everything it does or doesn't do in Zimbabwe.

Mbeki's view was that if he was too loud in his efforts President Robert Mugabe would merely stop paying attention to any diplomatic efforts, and thus there would be no restraining him. As a result, Mbeki refrained from ever criticising his Zimbabwean counterpart, even when it was clear that he was fixing elections in 2008 as hyperinflation ran at 500 billion percent (before the Zim dollar was scrapped).

While Mbeki was accused of being too close to Mugabe, the same charge cannot be laid at Zuma's door. Mugabe has been strongly critical of Zuma and his ANC. He has publicly insulted his envoy, Ambassador Lindiwe Zulu, and referred to Cyril Ramaphosa as a "white man in a black man's skin". In short, he can't stand Zuma. And the feeling would appear to be mutual, but if Zuma once had ambitions to sort out his northerly neighbour he quickly realised that his best option was to simply stand back and take Mugabe's shenanigans on the chin for fear of losing any last remaining influence he may have on him.

As Mbeki did before him, and as many other political leaders have done throughout the history of international relations, Zuma has effectively conceded that he can do nothing in what is a complex and extraordinarily tricky situation – because the only other real option is to declare war and invade. And as George W Bush might advise him, invasions generally don't tend to work out all that well.

So Zuma has had to placate Mugabe when he really doesn't want to. The fact that he is one of the best political operatives South Africa has ever produced is indicative of how difficult it is to deal with our neighbour.

To the complete lack of surprise of Zimbabwean political observers everywhere, the 89-year-old Mugabe strolled to a comfortable election victory in August 2013. The only doubt this time around was whether he even needed to fix anything to get the result. With the coalition government and despised enemy (and "ignoramus") Morgan Tsvangirai behind him, our mad uncle up north now has free rein to get up to whatever mischief he pleases.

Zuma, who sent him "profound congratulations" on his election victory – though they were probably a lot more "insincere" than "profound" – can only hope Mugabe doesn't cause too much damage to the region before he eventually goes to the big dictator palace up in the sky. At that point there will be an opportunity to more actively influence Zimbabwean politics again, and it will take some seriously first-class diplomatic skills to bring some kind of resolution to this regional problem. For now, the Zimbos in South Africa are here to stay. And serve you beer.

Blue-light brigades
Or: Motorcade madness; VIP security overkill
First erupted: early-2000s

For most people in Gauteng and KwaZulu-Natal it's a common site. A parade of black BMWs, with blue lights flashing and sirens blaring, blasting through traffic and often driving illegally in the process. All because one person, considered a VIP (Very Important Politician), is being transported from one place to another. Occupying the various support cars are that person's security personnel, who have no qualms breaking traffic laws, pushing people around and generally acting like they own the place. Which is possibly because they really believe they do.

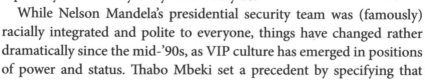

While Nelson Mandela's presidential security team was (famously) racially integrated and polite to everyone, things have changed rather dramatically since the mid-'90s, as VIP culture has emerged in positions of power and status. Thabo Mbeki set a precedent by specifying that his entourage include two separate cars carrying doctors, in case one of them was involved in the same accident he was in. Around the country, increasing numbers of ministers – some senior, others less so – worked out that your status was directly proportional to the number of black motor vehicles with blue lights in your immediate vicinity. Kgalema Motlanthe, in his brief time in charge, couldn't quite keep up with the trends – he often moved around with just three cars; his in the middle – but under Zuma, matters have escalated somewhat.

It now appears that almost every ANC provincial MEC has a set of guards who believe they are well within their rights to break the law. And speeding, reckless driving and generally offensive road behaviour are only the start of it. On the N12 near Johannesburg a motorist was assaulted for getting "too close" to a convoy. On the N3 near Durban a guard fired his gun out the window, while travelling at high speed, when a car didn't give way; it led to an accident that injured six people. In Ulundi a pedestrian was killed by a car travelling in Zuma's cavalcade. In Cape Town, another incident involving Zuma's team occurred when a student was arrested and held in a cell overnight after gesturing at the presidential motorcade while out jogging; he has brought a R1.45 million case against the state for kidnap and torture.

Many journalists covering ANC events can relate stories of being pushed around and confronted by groups of big angry men just because they took a picture of their nice BMW. It's hard to really contemplate the idiocy of this. Journalists are invited to watch the president in action; visiting a hospital, say. As he gets out of the car TV people and photographers crowd around as he thoroughly enjoys waving to them. But take a picture of the same car a few minutes later and suddenly you're committing treason...

"Nothing better symbolises the culture of entitlement that pervades the ruling party in South Africa than blue-light brigades."
– Dave Marrs, June 2013

In November 2012, a car transporting Gauteng housing MEC Humphrey Mmemezi jumped a red light and drove over Krugersdorp teenager Thomas Ferreira on his buzz bike. Ferreira was seriously injured and will likely never be the same again. Mmemezi had been late for a meeting. After Premier Nomvula Mokonyane visited the family to pay her condolences, she was interviewed on local radio as she drove away. Over the speed limit with her sirens on. Really. As she was quizzed about this amazingly inappropriate behaviour, she explained that for her "an emergency is when I'm late for a meeting". So that's official, then. Feel free to try that excuse for speeding for yourself the next time you have a pleasant conversation with a member of your local constabulary.

Journalists with long memories talk about how much less security there was around Parliament during the bad old days of apartheid compared to now. And that's not even counting the annual State of the Nation address, when all of central Cape Town is placed in lockdown and you're lucky to get in without having to leave a limb behind as a deposit. The justification for all of this is supposed to be "threat assessments" that are, supposedly, routinely undertaken by "the police". But it's hard to think it's not much more than a bit of VIP bling for those in power who enjoy showing that they're in power.

Public anger at these blue-light motorcades is growing; it used to be just middle-class whites venting their frustrations on the topic, but now everybody moans about them. The DA-controlled Western Cape has picked up on this and shrewdly banned them from its roads, looking for (and getting) an obvious thumbs-up from voters.

There have already been plenty of relatively minor incidents – though try telling that to Thomas Ferreira's family – and it's only a matter of time before one of these power-drunk VIP protection units actually ploughs into a bus, killing many people and causing a major scandal. Perhaps the people in the backseat could tell their drivers to slow down before we get there?

The police rot
Or: The lawless law;
why Marikana was allowed to happen
First emerged: early-2000s

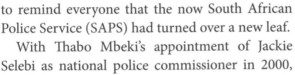

In the 1980s the police were held in such low regard as an organisation primarily designed to control – hence the phrase law and order – that they were simply not trusted by anyone living in a township. But after 1994, when they came under the Minister of Safety and Security, their image started to improve. They even added the word "service" to the end of South African Police (SAP) to remind everyone that the now South African Police Service (SAPS) had turned over a new leaf.

With Thabo Mbeki's appointment of Jackie Selebi as national police commissioner in 2000, however, things started to head downhill again. Selebi was thoroughly unfit for the job. Literally – he was overweight and out of shape – and figuratively – he had no police background at all and seemed barely aware that crime in South Africa even existed. Then when serious corruption charges against him first started emerging, Mbeki refused to act and told the nation to "trust me" on this. Anyone who did so was wrong.

Selebi was eventually convicted of taking money from convicted drugs trafficker Glenn Agliotti and, having spent a year and half without a police commissioner, it seemed life would start improving for the men and women in blue.

Well, no.

As Mbeki had appointed his good friend, so Jacob Zuma did the same thing. This time, in 2009, it was Bheki Cele, and immediately the tone of the leadership changed. Selebi started to militarise the police. Gone were the ranks of "inspector" and "superintendent" and in came

"What's all the fuss about crime?"

– Jacki Selebi, 2007

"Corporal" and "General". It was simply a giant step backwards. He also started to make comments that sounded a lot like encouragement to "shoot to kill", some of which were echoed by Zuma himself.

On the ground, police officers seemed to be getting more and more violent. Andries Tatane was killed by officers in a scene shown on TV. Around the country, complaints about police brutality and corruption became more and more common. As did stories of policemen murdering their wives and then killing themselves.

In the meantime the *Sunday Times* had found that Cele was planning to agree to a deal to move the SAPS headquarters into a building owned by a businessman, Roux Shabangu – and Shabangu, apparently connected to Zuma, would score to the tune of more than a billion rand over ten years.

Eventually Zuma was forced into a position where he had to let Cele go. Instead of replacing him with a career police officer, he appointed Riah Phiyega. Phiyega is an advocate, with many years of experience in the corporate and government environments. She's no police officer. And in a series of events that were both tragically unfair on her and showed her up completely, the Marikana shootings happened just days after her appointment. It was the deadliest police action against South African civilians since Sharpeville in 1960, and comparisons between the two were immediate and justified.

Phiyega tried to bolster her position within the police by telling the officers involved in the massacre that they had done the right thing, but she did her image in the eyes of the general public no good whatsoever in the process. The sense that the current South African Police Service was little more than a modern-day incarnation of the bad old apartheid force had taken hold.

Just when things couldn't get any worse, police officers were caught, again on camera, dragging Mozambican taxi driver Mido Macia behind their van. He was then beaten so badly that he died in a police cell. And while he was dying, no-one so much as lifted a finger to help him.

The police at the moment have lost their sense of legitimacy; as a result, they are hardly trusted by the public any more. In August 2013 it emerged that nearly 1,500 SAPS members were, according to a 2010 audit, convicted criminals, with crimes ranging from domestic violence and rape to housebreaking and murder. Our high-profile policemen from the last few years are the likes of Selebi, Cele, Richard Mdluli *(see p225)* and Robert McBride. Now Phiyega is out of her depth, doing a job she is not qualified for and probably didn't want in the first place.

It's dire times for our rotten police, and nothing short of a presidential decision to stop appointing political figures, but to simply pick the best police officer for the job from the start, will turn it around.

The dysfunctional NPA
Or: Why no-one trusts our criminal justice system
First emerged: early 2000s; first erupted: 2009

Controversies related to the National Prosecuting Authority date back long before Jacob Zuma became president. As the spy tapes saga suggests, it appears that the man Thabo Mbeki appointed as head of the NPA, Bulelani Ngcuka, had tried his best to interfere in the Zuma corruption case *(see p205).* So this is not just an issue that's sprung up because Zuma happens to be in charge – but the role he has subsequently played has certainly intensified the crisis.

The NPA is a critical institution. Its principle focus, as outlined in the Constitution, is directing criminal proceedings against people and entities

on behalf of the state – no small matter. So, you know, it's important that it runs well and transparently.

When Zuma came into office in 2009 he had to appoint a new NPA head. He chose the advocate Menzi Simelane. But there was a problem. An earlier commission had found that Simelane lied under oath while director-general of the Justice ministry. Notably, he had said that he believed the executive – that is the government, specifically the president – could make the final decision when it came to who gets prosecuted, rather than the head of the NPA. The Constitution is explicit that the president of the country cannot decide who should be prosecuted; the whole point of the NPA is that it is independent.

As it tends to do, the DA decided to go to court to challenge Simelane's appointment. Fast-forward a few years and eventually, in October 2012, the Constitutional Court ruled that Simelane was not a "fit and proper person" for the job and thus struck down his appointment. Consequently, the next appointment by Zuma to this post had to be someone who was "fit and proper".

Zuma, however, sidestepped this technicality by simply not appointing anyone. Eventually the Council for the Advancement of South Africa's Constitution lodged court papers, asking the Constitutional Court to force Zuma to make an appointment. In doing so, it pointed out that Zuma had said in an affidavit during an earlier legal battle that having a permanent head of the NPA was "in the national interest" and a "matter of urgency". He could hardly argue against himself, and he eventually had to give a legal undertaking to make an appointment.

In the meantime, the person who was running the NPA, advocate Nomgcobo Jiba, came under increasing scrutiny. She was charged with misconduct that alleged she'd tried to arrest a senior prosecutor to protect Jackie Selebi during his trial. At the same time it emerged that Zuma had pardoned her husband, who had been convicted of fraud, a move that now made him eligible for government jobs. She also made the questionable decision to charge Glynnis Breytenbach, the prosecutor investigating Richard Mdluli, which aroused suspicions that Mdluli was also being protected. *(See p225.)*

Over the months and years in which these little dramas have played out, the running of the NPA has, inevitably, been compromised. In fact, it has become more than a bit tragic. It was unable to convict any of the five police officers accused of killing protestor Andries Tatane in Ficksburg, despite the fact that everyone saw it happen on TV. When the long-running trial of the Fidentia fraudster J Arthur Brown finally concluded in early 2013, the NPA agreed to a plea bargain that saw him convicted on two counts, fined R150,000 and given a suspended jail sentence – this for a case involving hundreds of millions of rand that initially saw nearly 200 charges laid. As Judge Anton Veldhuizen unequivocally put it, "I think the state has mismanaged this… This is wrong." A perfect summation of the NPA in general, as more and more cases around South Africa have been postponed until the victims of wrongdoing simply give up on their quests for justice.

Fact is, the NPA has now lost the trust of much of the country, and with it has gone respect for the criminal justice system. When that happens in a place with a high crime rate like ours, people start taking the law into their own hands; vigilante justice emerges and a spiral starts that is very difficult to stop.

"In a constitutional democracy, an independent organ of state such as the NPA cannot delegate any of its constitutional powers to the president or his lawyers. Not in any matter. Never. Finish en klaar. Let alone in a private matter that has nothing to do with the Presidency but relates to the possible criminal prosecution of the person who happens to have been elected president."
– Pierre de Vos, 2013

Eventually, at the end of August 2013, Zuma finally appointed a new director of the NPA: Mxolisi Nxasana got the nod. He's an attorney from – you guessed it – KwaZulu-Natal, where he has been running his own practice for many years, and was once chair of the KwaZulu-Natal Law Society. Still in his mid 40s, he now has one of the most important jobs in the country. It may be unfair to him, but huge amounts of speculation will accompany his appointment, primarily as to whether he has made some kind of commitment to not charge Zuma with corruption, should the time come.

The Zuma spy tapes
Or: Zuma's get-out-of-jail-free card
First erupted: 2009

The Zuma spy tapes have all the intrigue of a good political thriller: corruption charges, spies, phone taps – all with the backdrop of forthcoming national elections.

After Schabir Shaik was convicted for his dodgy dealing with Zuma *(see p205)*, Zuma was charged with corruption by the National Prosecuting Authority. While it had been known for some time this would happen, he was finally served in December 2007, just a few days after he won the ANC leadership at Polokwane. Unsurprisingly, he brought several applications aimed at delaying any trial. As a result, by the beginning of 2009 it still hadn't started.

Meanwhile, an election was scheduled for April, and there was much public debate as to whether he would "run the country from the dock", or if the ANC would be forced to appoint someone else to the top job. Then, just a couple of weeks before the election, the NPA called a press conference in which its acting head, Mokotedi Mpshe, informed those present that he had decided to withdraw the corruption charges against Zuma because he had proof of interference in the decision to charge him in the first place.

Mpshe explained that Zuma's attorney, Michael Hulley, had informed him that a tape recording existed of a phone conversation between former NPA director, Bulelani Ngcuka, and Leonard McCarthy, then head of the Scorpions. In that conversation the two are understood to have conspired to charge Zuma with corruption at a time that would cause him the most embarrassment: just after Polokwane. Mpshe had sent two officials to the National Intelligence Agency to listen to these tapes, and was now convinced that this was clear evidence of interference. And so the charges against Zuma were withdrawn.

Here's the thing, though: while Mpshe did release a short transcript of the conversation, he did not release any audio recordings.

After the elections the DA decided to challenge Mpshe's decision in court. To do that it needed the information on which that decision was based, what the lawyers call a "record of the decision". Naturally, this included the taped conversations. But Hulley has refused to give up his copy (if he ever had one in the first place), while the NIA does the same. Eventually the Supreme Court of Appeal ruled that the NPA must provide this tape to the DA. Another High Court came to the same decision.

The suspicion here is that Zuma has ordered all the bodies under him, including the NIA, the NPA and Hulley, not to comply with this court order. Of course, this is not the type of conversation he will have had on email, so it's impossible to prove. But there are still many questions about whether the tapes were authentic, what they actually contain, and if they really were the basis for Mpshe's decision, or if his hand was simply forced somehow. He himself has become a travelling acting judge. If he were to be formally nominated as a permanent judge, he would face a public interview, where he would probably face questions about exactly this issue.

And so, if you believe Zuma to be the wiliest of political operators who knows how to duck and dive to cover his back, you may well conclude that Mpshe will end up being an acting judge for the rest of his career.

In the meantime, Zuma himself has appealed at every turn to make sure the tapes don't see the light of day. And yet, the tapes, in law, should help him. When pressed for answers, his officials won't give them.

(See Richard Mdluli, p225.)

The Protection of State Information Bill
Or: The Secrecy Bill; the Info Bill
First erupted: 2010

While Jacob Zuma's government is often blamed in its entirety for the huge public outcry that came about in reaction to the Protection of State Information Bill, this is, once again, a controversy that started with Thabo Mbeki. During Mbeki's time, it was realised there was something wrong with the current way our country deals with secrets. Actually, there was a whole lot wrong, considering it was the apartheid government that had promulgated the previous Act on the matter. So it was decided to sort it out once and for good. And yet, at the same time, the old (and equally apartheid-esque) National Key Points Act, which makes it illegal to take pictures of places we could tell you about but would have to kill you afterwards if we did (ahem, Nkandla), would stay in force. Not a promising start.

After several attempts, Zuma's government, led by that old information liberator State Security Minister Siyabonga Cwele, introduced the Protection of State Information Bill in 2010. There was silence at first. And then perhaps the biggest organised action by civil society since the HIV/Aids controversy. Various organisations bandied together under the banner of Right2Know, an umbrella group created specifically to fight what was quickly termed the Secrecy Bill. Key to its success was the political support of Cosatu which, as we know, is often the body to call on when you think the ANC is getting too big for its boots.

The problems with the Bill were numerous. Here are a couple of them.

First, and most crucially for its constitutionality, it allowed the minister of State Security to give literally any government official the power to classify information as "Top Secret". So if you ran a museum you had that power. If you were in charge of a municipality in trouble, hey, you had the power too. And if just wanted to do it for a laugh you could basically just whip out your big red stamp.

Next problem: once something was classified, you'd be in big, *big* trouble if it somehow came into your hands. The idea being that if you accidentally woke up with a box of Top Secret documents on your doorstep one morning, there would be a duty imposed upon you to take it to your nearest police station immediately. (Because Brixton Central was clearly set up to deal with this kind of thing.) And if you didn't do exactly that, you faced twenty years in jail. Cosatu, in particular, didn't like this element of the Bill because it meant that people who blew the whistle on corruption could be jailed. They declared it to be an existential threat to unions that would make it impossible for them to properly look after their members.

Add together just these two problems with the Bill and suddenly the avenues for hiding or covering up governmental corruption and incompetence would be vast and all too numerous.

The Bill's passage through Parliament saw national media editors walking out of the house in protest, demonstrations in front of newspaper offices, and some rip-roaring debates across all media and through every level of South African society. Government tried to justify it by saying it needed to control certain information in the interests of "state security". In response, its citizens laughed in its face (when they weren't angrily protesting). We're too cynical a nation to swallow that kind of excuse, especially when the man trying to force the Bill through Parliament has a wife whose day job happens to be drug dealing. (The Cweles were divorced in 2011, several months after Sheryl Cwele was convicted and sentenced to a lengthy jail term for trafficking drugs.) Without the moral authority to justify his plans, he couldn't defend them in public and had to rely on his officials to do so – unconvincingly – on his behalf. *(See p73.)*

Eventually, a slightly watered-down Bill was approved by Parliament in April 2013. But immediately – and this is the first time it's ever happened – every single opposition party declared in a joint statement their intention to go to the Constitutional Court to ask judges there to ratify it. In other words, they will now decide whether it's constitutional or not. This was a huge moment, considering that it had the right-wing Freedom Front Plus and the unbelievably left-wing Pan Africanist Congress agreeing on the same thing. In the final analysis, the biggest impact of this fight may be that it was the genesis of long-term cooperation between opposition parties.

Meanwhile the president himself appeared to delay signing the Bill into law. Which may mean his own lawyers were a bit worried about it. Another controversy with some space left to run…

Western Cape poo protests
Or: The DA's number one shitstorm; the toilet wars
First erupted: 2010

In India half of the population relieve themselves outside. In other words, one in every two Indians has no toilet in which to take a number one or a number two. And yet no-one in India, as far as we know, has ever tried to throw either a number one or a number two at any politician…

We really are different down here in South Africa, and especially in the Western Cape, because the throwing of faeces for political purposes is an increasingly common phenomenon. This in a

country where, as of 2012, nearly 95 percent of South Africans have access to working toilets.

It is a smelly business, of course, and the stench first started in the Makhaza area of Khayelitsha, Cape Town, in 2010, in the run-up to the local government elections of the following year. It was here that the DA-led government says it came to a deal with local residents, offering them either a certain number of fully enclosed toilets or a larger number of toilets without walls. If the residents took option number two (so to speak), the city would provide the materials to enclose the toilets, but it would be up to the residents to do the actual enclosing. The residents, on this version, chose option two.

In time, more than 1,300 toilets were installed, and the majority of them were quickly enclosed. But about 50 weren't. Those who used these facilities had to do so in plain view of everyone in the area, and often went about their business shamefully draped in a blanket. Eventually, members of the ANC Youth League in the area started to hold protests, with tensions escalating rapidly. First some toilets were destroyed; then they refused to allow the city to install prefabricated walls around the remaining toilets. In the end, the Western Cape High Court ruled against the DA, and forced them to enclose the toilets properly.

It was an issue that appeared to put the DA under very real political pressure, peaking

"The continuous throwing of human excrement does not only expose humans to bacterial infections such as E. coli, but [reduces] those throwing the poo in the streets to the same level as poo."
– Azanian People's Organisation statement, August 2013. (So far Azapo is possibly the only group to emerge smell-free...)

just before the elections. Helen Zille's mantra going into the polls was "service delivery, service delivery, service delivery", and the Makhaza protests seemed to prove that, actually, she wasn't delivering. For the first time, the DA was taking real heat as the party in power, a position it wasn't used to.

Then almost the same thing happened again – this time in a municipality in Viljoenskroon in the Free State, where hundreds of toilets had been built but not enclosed, and residents' rights to dignity were being violated on a daily basis. Zille could be forgiven for rejoicing ever so slightly on hearing this news, given that the municipality in question was ANC-run, and it would also be understood if she did a little jump for joy when it emerged that the company that was supposed to build the walls was partly owned by its mayor, Mantebu Mokgosi. You really could not make this shit up.

The rejoicing was short-lived, however, as the issue of sanitation in the Western Cape continued to fester. The City of Cape Town set up portable flush toilets inside dwellings, but without connections to the main sewer pipes. Now there were people doing number twos inside their homes, but the poo was sticking around until the council arrived to collect it.

Arguments immediately broke out about when and how often that was supposed to happen, and whether this setup was any better than the demeaning bucket system. Perhaps predictably, a small and militant band of ANC Youth League affiliates started to use this as ammunition. Literally. First an attack on Zille herself during an event, then a dumping on the steps of the Western Cape Legislature. And then the shit really flew inside Cape Town International Airport…

More than a dozen incidents occurred during the winter of 2013, often accompanied by the cordoning off of major roads. Claims that this was a political attempt to make the Western Cape "ungovernable" orchestrated by the ANC Youth League, and even condoned by the ANC itself, were given credence by the fact that there were newspaper people around to take pictures of many of the attacks – which meant they were being tipped off by the poo throwers themselves beforehand. According to an exasperated DA, the conspiracy even had a name: Operation Reclaim.

While the poo-flinging saga has put pressure on Zille, she has done her best to turn it back on the ANC, claiming it as proof that the party is stooping lower than anyone else. So far, she hasn't been proved wrong. The ANC itself says it disapproves of these protests, and will take action against any of its members found to be involved. It finally did so in September 2013, suspending seven people linked with poo-throwing incidents. Casual observers might suggest that it's taken them rather a long time to do so.

It remains to be seen who will win this odiferous war.

Richard Mdluli
Or: The nasty-looking police spy
First erupted: 2011

Richard Mdluli is a police officer who was, for a time, the head of Police Intelligence. It was a job that gave him the power to order phone taps and to keep people under surveillance. Over time it emerged that he was acquiring more and more power, and appeared to control the VIP guards that protect ministers.

Then, in 2011, it also emerged that he was the main suspect in the 1999 kidnapping and murder of a man who was married to a woman he was in a relationship with. At the same time, claims started to surface that the Police Intelligence slush fund was being looted and that Mdluli and people close to him were using that money to live the high life.

Though murder and fraud are no small charges, the most important claim against Mdluli, in a political context, was still to emerge: that he was listening to the phone calls of Jacob Zuma's political opponents. By this stage they were preparing for the ANC's Mangaung conference, and there was a widely held belief that Zuma was using Mdluli to spy on those who wanted to oust him.

They were so sure of this that some, like Fikile Mbalula, were actually prepared to say on record they believed their phones were being tapped. Mdluli had been a police officer since the late '70s and carried the reputation of being an apartheid stooge. Throw in a murder charge and it's fair to say that he was seen, in some quarters, as rather a bad bastard. As then acting ANC Youth League leader Ronald Lamola put it, "The DNA of Eugene de Kock flows through that man's veins."

Eventually Zuma was forced to remove Mdluli from his post, and transfer him to another. At the same time, a prosecutor investigating Mdluli, Glynnis Breytenbach, was suddenly accused of wrongdoing in a previous case she'd acted in. When she was acquitted of all of those charges, the public perception was that she had only been charged to keep her off the Mdluli case. If true – and it's a very logical conclusion – then this strengthens claims that Zuma has been using the police, and the National Prosecuting Authority, for his own ends.

Mdluli was put in limbo, and it seems he's too hot for Zuma to handle at the moment. As head of Police Intelligence, there is a widely held assumption that has come across the Zuma spy tapes at some point, but no-one has proof of this, and he isn't saying. You might speculate that he will maintain his silence and nothing will come of his murder charge.

> "Those were blue lies... That is part of those manufactured stories."
> – Richard Mdluli, testifying in court on charges of intimidation, kidnapping, assault, attempted murder, and conspiracy to commit murder

Nkandla
Or: Nkandlagate; Zumaville
First erupted: October 2012

political scheming
economic damage
corruption
incompetence
longevity
outcry

Geographically speaking, Nkandla is a part of rural KwaZulu-Natal, both a region and a town, about five hours' drive from Durban. But in our political circles it is shorthand for Jacob Zuma's home, which is situated there. And in media terms, it means scandal, corruption and public outcry.

The man at the centre of it all is, of course, our president, no stranger to *skandaal* and media storms in the last decade or so. And though Nkandla is far from the most damaging controversy to beset Zuma's career – either to him personally or to South Africa as a whole – it certainly appears to have taken top spot in the public perception since it emerged. This is possibly because it has come to personify the views of many critics of Zuma, both inside and outside the ANC. The gross looting of taxpayers' money, the none-too-subtle political obfuscation once details came to light, the patronage that appears to be condoned, the big man looking after his own with casual disregard for public opinion… More than that, though, there's a number on it: at least R206 million.

The controversy came to light on the back of a *Mail & Guardian* story in October 2012, in which it emerged that Zuma's home had been undergoing "renovations". Now, all of us have had to live in a house being fixed up from time to time. It's never pleasant. But for Zuma, it appears the term "renovations"

> "What do you do when President Obama or an African head of state visits him? You can't send them to a hotel."
> – Mac Maharaj, 2013

really meant "build your own village". And not a small one either.

Zuma's Nkandla "residence" – which is what you call it if you work for the SABC; it's a "compound" or a "homestead" if you're Helen Zille, and "a fortified country estate" in the words of *The New York Times* – comes complete with underground bunker, two (not one, mind you, two) astroturf soccer pitches for your guards, and a tuckshop for one of the wives to run. All of this is understandable for your average political leader. Problem is, it seems public money – in other words, your and my money – was used to build it. At least R206 million of that money, according to reports.

When the news of the amount first broke in the *City Press*, the Department of Public Works claimed the newspaper had its numbers wrong, and then, instead of investigating its own accounts, it tried to find the whistle-blower. They're still looking. Eventually Public Works minister Thulas Nxesi was forced to hold a press conference, and explain that the R206 million wasn't actually spent on building this little complex. Rather it was spent on providing proper security for the place, including bulletproof glass and that sort of thing. He then promptly announced an investigation into how those costs had escalated so quickly, and why they seemed to defy government handbook guidelines.

In Parliament, Zuma himself has claimed his family paid for the residence/compound/homestead itself, but it has not been shown how this was done. On current evidence he and his family simply don't have that kind of money, so the conclusion seems to be that someone must have paid his family so that they could pay for it. The identity of that someone would be very interesting to know.

The DA has claimed Nkandla as an example of bald corruption, plain and simple. Concerned observers within the Tripartite Alliance say it shows Zuma is being careless and making mistakes. But the most damaging real-term effects of Nkandla may be the way in which it has prevented law-enforcement agencies from really doing their job. Because of the very real fears that something might come out of it all, those investigating Nkandla have to tread incredibly carefully.

In terms of expenditure, whether corrupt or merely wasteful, the Nkandla numbers tend to pale somewhat against the estimated R2-billion town that has been mooted for construction a few kilometres down the road. Officially, the Umlalazi-Nkandla Smart Growth Centre, unofficially Zumaville, half of its build costs are likely to be funded with taxpayers' money. It may or may not happen. Nkandla, on the other hand, already has – and we haven't heard the last of it.

The Waterkloof invasion
Or: Guptagate
First erupted: 2013

On 29 April 2013 a Jet Airways Airbus A330 carrying more than 200 guests from India for a wedding of a member of the Gupta family landed at Waterkloof Air Force Base. It was clear immediately that the base was expecting them, and the red carpet had, quite literally, been laid out. Welcoming these people to South Africa, and obviously in charge of proceedings was Atul Gupta, one of the main movers in the Gupta family, who are known to be close to Jacob Zuma.

Even as a cavalcade transported the guests from the base on the outskirts of Pretoria to Sun City for the wedding, it began emerging that the Guptas had essentially used it for a personal social gathering. There was no legal or diplomatic reason for them to do so.

The outrage this evoked sprang up quicker than almost any other scandal in South African history. Practically every single group in society was furious, and they all started shouting at once. Even Gwede Mantashe at Luthuli House was forced to react. Instead of waiting to be driven to outrage, he led the charge, allowing other Alliance members to do the same. This seems to have been an attempt to take control of the situation, rather than allowing events to take control of the ANC.

The wedding itself went ahead. While several cabinet ministers had been invited and were expected to attend, most stayed away, realising that this was going to end badly. Zuma himself gave it a skip.

Government had to react, too, announcing an investigation into exactly what happened. But instead of any politicians being held to account or major heads rolling, all that happened was that Chief of State Protocol Bruce Koloane was suspended for his role in proceedings and then demoted a few months later and placed on probation. It seems that the entire scandal is going to be blamed on him. Oh, and they briefly suspended a couple of brigadier-generals and gave written warnings to nine Tshwane metro police officers who moonlighted for the private security firm that escorted the Gupta party to Sun City.

It appears no-one on the Gupta side of things was censured or fined in any way, and the Indian High Commission, meanwhile, claimed it had permission to use the base because several minor Indian provincial ministers were on board – which got people wondering if that perhaps stretched the bounds of diplomatic cordiality just a little.

The pertinent questions that emerged, however, all have to do with Zuma. What is his real relationship with the Guptas? Is he the "Number One" that Koloane referred to constantly while arranging permission for the landing? And what gave the Guptas the effrontery to try this stunt in the first place? Presumably they would have known beforehand that they would be protected from any consequences by a certain someone – and just who might that be…?

Along with Nkandla, the occupation of Waterkloof by a (foreign) private family has become a real symbol of a major criticism levelled against Zuma: that he is in debt to too many people, who then abuse government facilities and resources as a result. And, of course, it is yet another controversy for him to bear. Whether he will ever cave under the weight of them all remains to be seen.

Conclusion

If there is one lesson to learn from these pages it is this: in South African politics no-one ever stays on top for too long. For every action there is a not-necessarily-equal reaction. It is not a place where people will accept anyone with dictatorial tendencies; our history shows us there will, in the end, be some sort of rebellion.

This doesn't necessarily mean the ANC will be booted out of power; rather it shows that the ANC itself has to change over time. Whether or not it is successful in managing that difficult process will dictate whether it truly does stay in power until the time of the Rapture.

At the moment there are several large-scale processes playing out that will likely dictate the future of our politics. The first is the diminishing role of racial politics. Your race no longer necessarily determines how you vote. Historically, the interests of a class of people tend to be more important to those people than their racial identities. But it's a complex process, and it's different for everyone. Someone who grew up in an "ANC family" is unlikely to vote DA just because they went to Houghton Primary. But someone who grew up in Potchefstroom may vote blue because they don't like their local ANC councillor.

In most places choices are really economic. "It's the economy, stupid," was what Bill Clinton taught the world (along with a few less savoury phrases). If economic growth continues to slow, then the ANC could come under more pressure. It also faces huge problems making decisions about the economy because it is trying to accommodate the capitalist class of Cyril Ramaphosa and Tokyo Sexwale on the one side, and the communists and unionists on the other. This means every time it moves slightly to the right – towards, say, making it easier to hire and fire – there is a reaction to that, and the leader of the ANC is weakened. So at the moment it is not really in his short-term interests to do what could be in the long-term economic interests of the country. The ANC would say that it still has to defend the working class.

But that's politics.

A brief look at the longer-term economic trends shows that the economy is growing, more and more people are better educated than they've ever been, and almost everyone has some sort of access to water and electricity. But there are still too many young people without jobs, who have now given up hope of ever getting one.

These are the people who our current political system are leaving behind. Having said that, the longer-term trends show that our country is getting better, and will continue to do so. The global trend towards greater transparency will not leave us untouched, and it will become harder for politicians of any stripe to keep secrets hidden. At the same time Africa itself is changing, becoming more democratic and wealthier. This will affect us too.

In our politics change happens slowly, and then very quickly. It's just predicting the change itself that is difficult. But expect more openness, less corruption and more pressure on politicians. And expect them to have to react to that in order to survive.

Further reading

We've covered a lot of ground in less than 240 pages. There are many excellent books on South African politics to take you further. I recommend the following for more detailed explorations on –

Cyril Ramaphosa – a lucid biography of the man who would be king. *Cyril Ramaphosa* by Anthony Butler (Jacana, updated edition 2013).

Jacob Zuma – including all the inside dirt on the scandals that matter, written by someone who really knows. *Zuma Exposed* by Adriaan Basson (Jonathan Ball, 2012).

The evolution of South African politics under the Zuma presidency – hugely detailed and insightful, by an author who understands better than almost anyone the structure of the state and the ANC politics that underpin it. *The Zuma Years: South Africa's Changing Face Of Power* by Richard Calland (Zebra, 2013).

The Arms Deal – the inside story from a former ANC MP who was actually there. *After The Party* by Andrew Feinstein (Jonathan Ball, 2007). Or, for the overview, try *The Devil In The Detail* by Paul Holden and Hennie van Vuuren (Jonathan Ball, 2011).

Politics outside of the ANC – proof that the ANC wasn't *everything* during the struggle. *Biko: A Biography* by Xolela Mangcu (Tafelberg, 2012).

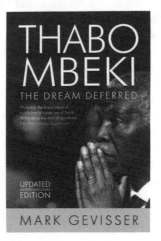

The ANC before 1990 (and Thabo Mbeki) – Mbeki's authoritative biography and still a must-read for anyone interested in the history of the ANC and South Africa. *The Dream Deferred* by Mark Gevisser (Jonathan Ball, 2009, updated edition).

Glossary

Agang Brand-spanking-new political party led by Mamphela Ramphele – *p199*

ACDP African Christian Democratic Party – *p191*

The Alliance Short for Tripartite Alliance.

AMCU Association of Mineworkers and Construction Union – *p166*

ANC African National Congress. Liberation movement, governing party – *p118*

Anti-majoritarianism Pejorative term used to criticise those who resist constitutional changes – *p29*

The Arms Deal One of the largest and longest-running post-apartheid corruption scandals, involving the 1999 procurement of armaments – *p205*

Block, John Controversial ANC provincial leader in Northern Cape – *p106*

Brown, J Arthur Former Fidentia boss, convicted of fraud – *p217*

Buthelezi, Mangosuthu Ageing leader of the IFP – *p190*

Cabinet The most senior level of the executive branch of government – *p70*

Carrim, Yunus Minister of Communications – *p81*

Cele, Bheki Former national police commissioner, dismissed in 2011 following corruption allegations – *p213*

Chabane, Collins Minister in the Presidency, responsible for Performance Monitoring and Evaluation – *p98*

Chapter Nines Constitutional institutions mandated to protect various rights, often against government – *p170*

Codesa talks Convention for a Democratic South Africa. Transition negotiations that led to 1994 elections – *p20*

The Constitution Supreme law of the Republic of South Africa, revered by some, contested by others – *p20*

Constitutional Court Highest court in South Africa – *p23*

Cope Congress of the People. Briefly serious ANC breakaway party, imploded in infighting and disaster – *p195*

Cosatu Congress of South African Trade Unions. Union federation and voice of 2.2 million workers. One-third of the Tripartite Alliance – *p161*

Cronin, Jeremy Deputy minster of Public Works, and first deputy general secretary of the SACP – *p159*

Cwele, Siyabonga Minister of State Security, spy boss, ex-husband of drugs trafficker – *p73*

DA Democratic Alliance. The official opposition – *p178*

Davies, Rob Minister of Trade and Industry – *p99*

De Klerk, FW Seventh and last president of apartheid-era South Africa.

Dlamini, Bathabile Minister of Social Development – *p94*

Dlamini-Zuma, Nkosazana Chair of the African Union, possible future president of South Africa – *p146*

Duarte, Jessie Deputy secretary-general of the ANC – *p143*

EFF Economic Freedom Fighters. Malema's crowd – *p197*

FF+ Freedom Front Plus. Conservative

right-wing party – *p192*

Fransman, Marius ANC provincial leader in the Western Cape – *p106*

Freedom Charter Statement of core principles of the South African Congress Alliance (ANC, SACP) issued in 1955.

Freedom Under Law Non-profit organisation that promotes democratic values in the judicial system – *p53*

Gauntlett, Jeremy Highly regarded white advocate repeatedly rejected by the JSC for judicial positions – *p53*

GEAR Growth, Employment and Redistribution Programme. 1996 macroeconomic policy, heavily criticised by Cosatu – *p153*

Gigaba, Malusi Minister of Public Enterprises – *p90*

Gordhan, Pravin Respected and influential Minister of Finance – *p74*

Green Paper First draft of a policy to become a White Paper and thus law – *p42*

The Guptas Indian family, including brothers Atul, Ajay and Rajesh. Industrialists, newspaper and TV-station owners, Waterkloof users, Zuma friends – *p229*

Hanekom, Derek Minister of Science and Technology – *p93*

Hefer Commission Inquiry set up to investigate allegations of spying against Bulelani Ngcuka – *p68*

Holomisa, Bantu Leader of the UDM, with small Xhosa following – *p194*

Hulley, Michael Zuma's lawyer – *p219*

IEC Independent Electoral Commission. Runs all national, provincial and local elections – *p31*

IFP Inkatha Freedom Party. Once-influential party, based in KZN – *p190*

Info Bill Short for Protection of State Information Bill.

Joemat-Pettersson, Tina Minister of Agriculture, Forestry and Fisheries – *p79*

JSC Judicial Service Commission. Body that appoints SA judges. Current focal point of government's constitutional power struggles – *p50*

Koloane, Bruce Chief of state protocol during Waterkloof controversy – *p230*

Kiviet, Noxolo Premier of the Eastern Cape – *p104*

Lekota, Mosiuoa Leader of Cope – *p195*

Leon, Tony Former DA leader – *p179*

Lucas, Sylvia Premier of the Northern Cape – *p104*

Luthuli House Headquarters of (and shorthand for) the ANC – *p112*

Mabuza, David Premier of Mpumalanga – *p105*

Madonsela, Thuli Influential, highly regarded public protector – *p111*

Magashule, Ace Premier of the Free State – *p104*

Maharaj, Mac High-profile spokesman for the Presidency – *p66*

Mahumapelo, Supra Provincial leader in the North-West province – *p104*

Maimane, Mmusi Up-and-coming national spokesman of the DA – *p188*

Malema, Julius Somewhat controversial former ANCYL leader, current EFF leader, future fraud convictee (probably). Claimed to play role in ascent to power by Zuma. Expelled by Zuma – *p197*

Mandela, Nelson Our hero – *p13*

Mangaung Venue of ANC's 53rd national

conference, held in December 2012, at which Zuma easily defeated Kgalema Motlanthe for party presidency – *p58*

Mantashe, Gwede Hugely powerful secretary-general of the ANC – *p136*

Manuel, Trevor Minister in the Presidency, in charge of the National Planning Commission. Known for his lengthy tenure as Minister of Finance – *p96*

Mapisa-Nqakula, Nosiviwe Minister of Defence and Military Veterans – *p83*

Marikana Site of infamous massacre in August 2012, involving police firing on striking workers at Lonmin mine. In total 44 people died and 78 were injured. Compared to Sharpeville – *p214*

Martins, Ben Minister of Energy – *p84*

Mashatile, Paul ANC provincial leader in Gauteng – *p80*

Masualle, Phumulo ANC provincial leader in the Eastern Cape – *p104*

Mathabatha, Stan Premier of Limpopo – *p104*

Mathale, Cassel Former premier of Limpopo – *p105*

Mathunjwa, Joseph AMCU president – *p166*

Mazibuko, Lindiwe Up-and-coming DA leader in Parliament – *p187*

Mbalula, Fikile Minister of Sport and Recreation. Ex-Zuma fan – *p95*

Mbeki, Thabo Ex-president of South Africa, fired by ANC in 2008. Ex-Zuma friend – *p64*

Mbete, Baleka ANC chairwoman – *p140*

McBride, Robert One-time ANC bomber and Ekurhuleni Metro police chief. Received jail sentence for drunken driving, acquitted on appeal – *p215*

McCarthy, Leonard Former Scorpions boss. Has speaking part in Zuma spy tapes – *p218*

Mchunu, Senzo ANC provincial leader in KwaZulu-Natal – *p105*

MDC Movement for Democratic Change. Official Zimbabwean opposition – *p209*

Mdluli, Richard Controversial (and scary) former head of Police Intelligence – *p225*

MEC Member of the Executive Council. Part of provincial Executive Councils, which consist of the premier and five to ten MECs, each with their own specific portfolios – *p46*

Meyer, Ivan DA provincial leader in the Western Cape – *p106*

Mkhize, Zweli ANC treasurer and former KwaZulu-Natal premier – *p142*

Modise, Joe Former Minister of Defence. Widely implicated in Arms Deal corruption allegations – *p205*

Modise, Thandi Premier of the North-West – *p106*

Mogoeng, Mogoeng Chief justice in the Constitutional Court. Appointed under controversial circumstances in 2011 – *p54*

Mokonyane, Nomvula Premier of Gauteng – *p104*

Molewa, Edna Minister of Water and Environmental Affairs – *p101*

Moseneke, Dikgang Progressive deputy chief justice. Highly regarded by peers, but unloved by government – *p52*

Motlanthe, Kgalema Current deputy president of South Africa. Former ANC deputy president, replaced by Cyril Ramaphosa at Mangaung. Significant loss of power since then. Oh, and former president of South Africa – *p56*

Motshekga, Angie Minister of Basic Education. Face of the Limpopo textbook disaster – *p80*

Motsoaledi, Aaron Highly regarded Health minister – *p76*

MP Member of Parliament – *p40*

Mpshe, Mokotedi Former director of public prosecutions for the Justice department. Linked to Zuma spy tapes saga – *p218*

Mthembu, Jackson ANC spokesman – *p145*

Mthethwa, Nathi Minister of Police – *p89*

Mulder, Pieter FF+ leader – *p192*

Mushwana, Lawrence Not particularly impressive chairman of the SAHRC – *p107*

National Assembly Workhorse of Parliament, where national laws are debated. Made up of 400 elected MPs decided by proportional representation – *p41*

National Key Points Act Apartheid-era legislation that classifies certain state entities of strategic importance. Used as Nkandla smokescreen – *p220*

National Working Committee Group of up to 26 senior ANC members that meets regularly to carry out NEC instructions – *p129*

NCOP National Council of Provinces. House of Parliament responsible for provincial legislation and interests – *p39*

Ndebele, S'bu Minister of Correctional Services – *p82*

NEC National Executive Committee. The power core of the ANC, totalling the party's top six officials plus 80 members voted at its most recent conference. In essence, the people who run SA – *p127*

NFP National Freedom Party. IFP offshoot – *p196*

Ngcuka, Bulelani Former national director of public prosecutions. Other star of Zuma spy tapes – *p218*

Nkandla Jacob Zuma's residence/homestead in central KwaZulu-Natal. Also the related scandal involving a reported R206 million security upgrade at taxpayers' expense – *p227*

Nkoana-Mashabane, Maite Minister of International Relations and Cooperation – *p86*

Nkwinti, Gugile Minister of Rural Development and Land Reform – *p93*

NPA National Prosecuting Authority – *p215*

NUM National Union of Mineworkers. Cosatu's largest affiliate, with more than 300,000 members – *p165*

NUMSA National Union of Metalworkers of South Africa. Similarly large and powerful affiliate of Cosatu – *p167*

Nxesi, Thulas Minister of Public Works – *p92*

Nzimande, Blade Minister of Higher Education, general secretary of the SACP, BMW driver – *p156*

Oliphant, Mildred Minister of Labour – *p87*

Operation Vula ANC operation set up to smuggle freedom fighters into South Africa in the '80s. Key players included Zuma, Maharaj and Gordhan.

Outa Opposition to Urban Tolling

Alliance. Civic action group of business associations and individuals, formed to challenge government's decision to implement e-tolling in Gauteng – *p186*

Pandor, Naledi Minister of Home Affairs – *p85*

Parastatals State-owned enterprises, often mired in controversy, including Eskom, Telkom, Transnet, SAA etc – *p114*

Parliament The highest assembly of elected political representatives, where government happens – *p39*

Patel, Ebrahim Minister of Economic Development – *p84*

Peters, Dipuo Minister of Transport – *p100*

Phiyega, Riah National police commissioner, appointed following the dismissal of Bheki Cele – *p214*

Phosa, Mathews Former ANC treasurer – *p126*

Polokwane Venue of the ANC's 52nd national conference, held in December 2007. Watershed moment in SA politics when Zuma overthrew Mbeki – *p60*

Protection of State Information Bill Legislation intended to keep government "secrets" way too secret. Highly contested and eventually watered down – *p220*

Provincial legislature Provincial branch of government from which MECs and NCOP members are elected – *p103*

Pule, Dina Former Communications minister, fired in 2013 and currently under investigation for funnelling government contracts and resources to her boyfriend. Bad apologiser – *p84*

Radebe, Jeff Minister of Justice and Constitutional Development – *p77*

Ramaphosa, Cyril Deputy president of the ANC. Hope of the middle class, possible future president – *p132*

Ramphele, Mamphela Leader of Agang, mother of Steve Biko's children – *p199*

Rand Rebellion Armed uprising of white miners in 1922 – *p150*

Rooi gevaar "Red danger". Apartheid government's colloquial name given to its feared communist threat – *p149*

SACP South African Communist Party. The *rooi gevaar* in action – *p149*

SAHRC South African Human Rights Commission. Chapter Nine institution that investigates human rights violations – *p107*

SARS South African Revenue Service. The taxman. Probably the most efficiently run government department of them all.

Scorpions Also known as the Directorate of Special Operations (DSO). Unit within the NPA tasked with tackling high-level crime. Controversially disbanded by the ANC in 2008.

Secrecy Bill Nickname for Protection of State Information Bill.

Selebi, Jackie Former national police commissioner, convicted of corruption in 2010 – *p216*

September, Connie Minister of Human Settlements – *p86*

Shabangu, Susan Minister of Mineral Resources – *p88*

Shaik, Schabir Associate of Jacob Zuma, imprisoned for 15 years on charges of corruption and fraud relating to Arms Deal bribes that involved, and seemingly implicated, Zuma. Released on medical parole in 2009. Still alive – *p207*

Shilowa, Mbhazima Former premier of Gauteng and deputy president of Cope. Not prominent in book – *p195*

Shivambu, Floyd Some dude.

Simelane, Menzi Former NPA director appointed by Zuma. Removed from his position by Constitutional Court ruling as unfit appointee – *p27*

Sisulu, Lindiwe Minister of Public Service and Administration – *p91*

Slovo, Joe Long-time leader of the SACP and senior member of the ANC during transition period – *p152*

The Spear Controversial painting of semi-naked Jacob Zuma – *p80*

Suppression of Communism Act Legislation passed by apartheid government in 1950 that criminalised all communist activity – *p151*

Tatane, Andries Citizen killed by police during service delivery protest – *p214*

Tripartite Alliance Conflicted grouping of the ANC, SACP and Cosatu – *p172*

TRC Truth and Reconciliation Commission

Tsenoli, Lechesa Minister of Cooperative Governance and Traditional Affairs – *p82*

Tshabalala-Msimang, Manto Former Health minister, tasked with pushing Mbeki's disastrous HIV/Aids policies. Also known as Dr Beetroot – *p76*

UDF United Democratic Front. Major anti-apartheid movement of the '80s.

UDM United Democratic Movement. Once-influential party, based in Eastern Cape – *p194*

United Party Ruling party in South Africa between 1934 and 1948. Merger between the National Party, the South African Party and the Unionist Party.

Van Schalkwyk, Marthinus Minister of Tourism. Final leader of the (New) National Party – *p98*

Vavi, Zwelinzima High-profile leader of Cosatu. Had a newsworthy 2013 – *p169*

Waterkloof Air Force base near Pretoria. Also the related scandal involving the Gupta family's use thereof – *p229*

White Paper Final version of legislation before it becomes a Bill. Compare Green Paper – *p42*

Xingwana, Lulu Minister of Women, Children and People with Disabilities – *p101*

Yengeni, Tony Former ANC chief whip, jailed briefly for taking Arms Deal bribe. In the news for driving habits.

Youth wage subsidy Proposed legislation to incentivise companies to employ graduates by subsidising their salaries. Rejected by Cosatu.

Zanu-PF Zimbabwe African National Union – Patriotic Front. Ruling party of Zimbabwe for 30+ years.

Zille, Helen Leader of the DA and premier of the Western Cape – *p183*

Zuma rape trial High-profile court case that saw Zuma investigated on charges of rape in 2006, and eventually acquitted on all charges. Source of shower cartoons.

Zuma spy tapes Classified recordings related to Arms Deal controversy – *p218*

Zuma, Jacob President of the ANC and the Republic of South Africa – *p57*

Listen to Stephen Grootes, host of the Midday Report,
12-1pm weekdays on
Talk Radio 702 and **567 CapeTalk**

Follow Stephen Grootes on Twitter
@StephenGrootes